GW00368145

The Storytellers

A glimpse into the lives
of 12 English writers

This England

First published in 1991
by This England Books,
73 Rodney Road, Cheltenham, Gloucestershire

Printed in Great Britain by

BPCC Wheatons Ltd, Exeter

Copyright This England 1991

All rights reserved. No part of this publication
may be reproduced, stored in a retrieval system,
or transmitted, in any form or by any means,
electronic, mechanical, photocopying, recording
or otherwise without first having the permission
of the publishers.

ISBN 0 906324 20 3

CONTENTS

INTRODUCTION

I f you are old enough to recall the BBC *Children's Hour* broadcasts any time from the mid-Thirties up to the darkest days of the last world war, there will be at least one segment in that most enjoyable programme that still clings to memory . . . "Out with Romany", which invited young listeners to accompany a mellow-voiced gypsy of that name, and his dog Raq, on weekly journeys of adventure into the countryside. The half-hour slot was introduced by a haunting melody which I can hear now in the sound archives of my mind. It was called *Lullaby of the Leaves* and it set the scene for 30 minutes of wonderment and imagery which transported youngsters like myself away from the realities of the day, grim as they sometimes were, to a world of Nature, wild life and discovery. "Romany" — the son of a Salvation Army preacher and a gypsy mother — rambled his way into the nation's heart in those far-off days. In real life he was a Methodist minister by the name of the Rev. George Bramwell Evens who also produced a series of interesting books based on those early wireless programmes which stretched for 10 years from 1933 to 1943.

Many years later, while researching articles for *This England* magazine, I began tracing Romany's roots and located his caravan which can still be found at Wilmslow in Cheshire. With the valuable assistance of his daughter Roma, and aided by a fellow listener to those *Children's Hour* programmes, David Lazell, the remarkable story of Romany was pieced together. It proved to be only one of a series of features into the lives of many English authors and poets who deserve to be better known among a far wider audience. My continuing journey along this path led to the tiny village of Juniper Hill in North Oxfordshire, and to a thatched cottage by a meadow . . . this was the house and the hamlet where little Flora Thompson was born and brought up, and which inspired her to write the heart-warming trilogy *Lark Rise to Candleford.* Flora wrote with such great feeling, for she knew poverty in childhood, despair as a wife, and grief as a mother. Like Mary Webb of Shropshire, whose sad story is also told in this book, she never knew real fame in her own lifetime. One who did was the remarkable Flora

Klickmann, editress of *The Girl's Own Paper*, a legend among periodicals earlier this century. Flora would leave her Fleet Street office on Friday afternoon and steam westward by train to the tiny railway station at Tintern, on the Monmouthshire side of the River Wye. From there she would walk across the iron-latticed bridge to the neighbouring village of Brockweir

on the Gloucestershire side of the river, and within a hundred yards or so arrived at her stone cottage and stepped into the dream world called "Flower Patch Country". This land of literary fancy inspired a whole series of her books and even a regular magazine which flourished for many years.

Other researches took me to the southernmost point of the Isle of Wight, where the poet-philosopher Alfred Noyes — blind in his old age — lived and worked; to the streets of Halesowen in Worcestershire where the tall and angular Francis Brett Young practised as a family doctor in between writing his novels, some of which were later turned into successful films; to London and the Home Counties delving into the backgrounds of Arthur Mee, surely England's finest editor, and that ebullient giant of literature, G.K. Chesterton, who championed the common man in prose and poetry; and to the South Coast to retrace the steps of a Hastings doctor's daughter, Sheila Kaye-Smith, whose Sussex novels await discovery by a whole new generation of readers.

Part of the enjoyment in researching and writing the articles that have now been collected to form this volume, has been in knowing that even though some of their work may be recalled with affection, or ring bells in the distant past, many people will know little or nothing about the lives of those included here. Shakespeare, Milton, Dickens and Hardy are among the giants of English prose and poetry whose lines and lives have been minutely chronicled and debated in great detail. It is partly to counter the decades of virtual neglect suffered by those in the lesser ranks of literature that we have selected twelve storytellers whose own stories are worth the telling.

SIMON APPLEYARD

G.K. Chesterton, the journalist, novelist, poet and gifted debater, who was a literary giant in every sense.

G.K. CHESTERTON

(1874-1936)

Champion of the Common Man

Hymnwriters have often claimed that unusual circumstances gave them the inspiration to write their sacred verses and one man can claim to have written his hymn as a result of a crime story. For had it not been for a brisk walk across the Yorkshire moors in 1903, Gilbert Keith Chesterton might never have met the mild-mannered, but astute parish priest who later became immortalised as "Father Brown".

Lovers of detective stories will know all about this self-effacing country cleric with a shabby umbrella who leads police to capture the world's most dangerous fictional criminal, the inimitable Flambeau. But not all will perhaps realise that he was modelled on a real-life friend of the Chestertons — a witty and sprightly Yorkshireman with an Irish name — Father John O'Connor, a curate at St. Anne's R.C. Church at Keighley, Yorkshire. The young priest not only inspired Chesterton to write the detective series, which at one time seemed likely to topple even Sherlock Holmes in popularity, but he also provided a resilient wall of faith against which Chesterton could bounce the ball of his own Christian ideals and theories. This led the brilliant young writer on a tortuous journey from radical agnosticism to full-blooded orthodox Christianity, one outcome of which was his well-known hymn. Not only did it fight the good fight at a time when popular opinion was turning more towards atheism, but it also attacked the materialism of the era (as expressed in the words "the walls of gold entomb us"), the emergent Marxist cause espoused by power-seekers, and the continuing divisions within the Christian fold itself.

The hymn — No. 308 in *Songs of Praise* — is listed as

Hymn

O God of earth and altar
Bow down and hear our cry,
Our earthly rulers falter,
Our people drift and die;
The walls of gold entomb us,
The swords of scorn divide,
Take not thy thunder from us,
But take away our pride.

From all that terror teaches,
From lies of tongue and pen,
From all the easy speeches
That comfort cruel men,
From sale and profanation
Of honour and the sword,
From sleep and from damnation,
Deliver us, good Lord!

Tie in a living tether
The prince and priest and thrall,
Bind all our lives together,
Smite us and save us all;
In ire and exultation
Aflame with faith, and free,
Lift up a living nation,
A single sword to thee.

G.K.C.

Chesterton at the age of 16, by which time he had read all the works of Shakespeare and most of the novels of Dickens — and he didn't learn to read until he was nine!

When Chesterton was asked what books he would most like to have with him if he were stranded on a desert island, he replied: "Thomas's Guide to Practical Shipbuilding."

being sung to the tune "King's Lynn", a traditional English melody, but these days it is more often sung to the better-known tune "Aurelia", which is also used for *The Church's one foundation*. Chesterton gave it the simple title of "Hymn" and included it in his collected verse published in 1915, but it was obviously written several years earlier than that.

Because of his positive attitude and opinion on many issues of the day, Chesterton opened himself to attack from a variety of quarters. He became renowned in print and on the wireless, where he endeared himself to millions in his weekly broadcast talks, as a champion of the little man. And he never lost a verbal battle or came off second best in a debate.

Such was the prowess of this larger than life figure who confronted and confounded some of the important figures of the times — George Bernard Shaw, H.G. Wells and Bertrand Russell among them. His rotund, 20-stone bulk — clad in cloak and broad black hat, bearing a drooping moustache, *pince nez* spectacles, and carrying a sword-stick — made Chesterton a legend in Fleet Street, where he could often be seen in shop doorways composing poetry on the back of an envelope, or jotting down an idea on the cuff of his shirt!

Yet few people could have prophesied his success from the modest beginnings of life. Born in Campden Hill, Kensington, on May 29th, 1874, the elder son of a London estate agent (the family name lives on still, as "Chestertons") he was a backward pupil at St. Paul's School which he attended as a day boy, being two years behind his age group. He couldn't read until the age of nine. A year later he had grown as tall as most men, yet still his mother dressed him in the customary child's sailor suit. The combination of his bulk, a thin squeaky voice, and backwardness at school, compelled his parents to take him to a brain specialist, and his mother later said the doctor told her that Gilbert had the largest brain he had ever come across, and that "he would grow up to be either an imbecile or a genius". Only after a visit to an optician, who discovered severe short-sightedness, did the young Gilbert begin his climb to literacy, and within six years he read all of Shakespeare, many of the Classics, much of Dickens and dozens of "penny dreadfuls".

Chesterton believed in "prolonged childhood" — not allowing children to grow old before their time. Indeed,

The front of St. Paul's School in London, which Chesterton attended as a day boy.

throughout his long and eventful life as a journalist, author and broadcaster, during which he visited many countries and mixed with the highest names in the land, he later confessed that his experiences meant far less to him than the Punch and Judy show he enjoyed as a child in Campden Hill. The singing of hymns, or traditional English songs, was well ingrained in Chesterton's psyche, for as a child he recalled his paternal grandfather keeping up the ancient Christian custom of singing at the dinner table.

While at St. Paul's he and his school-friends formed a Junior Debating Club, and it was here that Chesterton's skill as an orator and verbal thinker first showed itself. Among the members of that youthful fraternity was E.C. Bentley, who became Chesterton's life-long friend. Bentley's middle name was Clerihew, and he it was who invented the four-line comic verse form which bears that title, thus putting his name in the English Dictionary forever:

> *Sir Humphrey Davy*
> *Abominated gravy.*
> *He lived in the odium*
> *Of having discovered sodium.*

Chesterton was already showing signs of the poetry that was in him. By the age of 17 he had seen his earlier verses in print and won the school's prestigious Milton Prize for poetry. The following year, all his friends went up to Oxford to continue their studies, but Chesterton chose instead the Slade School of Art, since he had determined to become an artist. It was while there that he felt, within

In 1930 I was a pupil at a convent "finishing school" in Rome. G.K. Chesterton sometimes came to visit our Reverend Mother; we knew him by sight, and, once seen, who could forget the huge man in the big, black cloak? Part of our "finishing" process was to be taken round the museums and galleries of the Eternal City. One day we were being shepherded through the Vatican Museum. My friend and I somehow managed to get separated from the rest of our party and in one of the galleries whom should we see but Mr. G.K. Chesterton. He was about to leave so we followed him down the stairs in the hope of being able to get his autograph. At the foot of the stairs he turned. "As we had such young legs", he said, "could one of us be so kind as to run back to the gallery where he had left his cloak, and would the other see if she could find him a carrozza?" We needed no second bidding. I raced back up the stairs, found the familiar black cloak where he had left it and triumphantly returned it to its owner. Meanwhile my friend had found a vacant carrozza. G.K. thanked us both, climbed into the carrozza and drove off. In the excitement we had forgotten about the autographs. Next day a letter arrived at our convent. He addressed it to "The Young Ladies suffering education at the convent at No.10 Via Boncompagni". Inside was a sheet full of autographs and a little poem.

> *To be a real prophet once*
> *For you alone did I desire,*
> *Who brought the prophet's mantle down*
> *And called his chariot of fire!*

I have the precious autograph still and what a strange Chinese-looking affair it is! — MRS. L. RIPLEY, BRIGHTON, SUSSEX.

(Part of a letter published in the Winter 1986 issue of *This England*)

When Chesterton's popular Father Brown novels appeared on television, it was that marvellous actor Kenneth More (above) who delighted audiences with his portrayal of the priest-detective. Chesterton based his hero on a real-life priest, Father John O'Connor (below) of Keighley in Yorkshire.

himself, the enveloping pessimism and evil gloom of being a modern atheist and radical thinker. He stopped short, examined the facts of Creation, and almost on the spot and for the rest of his life became a committed Christian.

This was now 1894; Chesterton was only 20, but he plunged once again into a heavy bout of reading — the Bible, Walt Whitman and Robert Louis Stevenson — and gave up art training for a job in publishing, where he began reading manuscripts and had a shot at editing. By 1899 he had met the girl he intended to marry — Frances Blogg. When his employers refused to double his salary, so enabling him to wed, Chesterton resigned on the spot and devoted himself to full-time writing. Within a year he had two books of poetry published, one of which included "*The Donkey*", perhaps his most famous verse for children. His declared opposition to the Boer War caused him to be given several writing commissions by Fleet Street newspapers, and in 1901 he and Frances were married at Kensington parish church. A glimpse of his legendary absent-mindedness showed itself even on his wedding day — he turned up at the church without his tie (a friend went to a nearby shop to buy one just before the bride arrived!) and on the way to Liverpool Street station to catch the express to Ipswich for the honeymoon, he stopped off for a glass of milk — and they missed the train!

In 1903 came his first major book success, a biography of Robert Browning, and this — coupled with his growing stature as a columnist in the daily Press — brought him increased literary notice. He undertook frequent lecture tours, particularly in the North of England, and it was on one such to Yorkshire that he met the prototype for his "Father Brown". The sharp-witted priest remained close friends with the Chestertons for life, yet never tried to influence them with his own religion, and it was to be another 19 years before G.K. asked the little priest from Yorkshire to come down to his house in Beaconsfield, Bucks, to receive him into the Catholic Church.

That was in 1922 when Chesterton was at the height of his fame — he had produced his most famous novel *The Man Who Was Thursday* in 1908 and dedicated it to his old friend E.C. Bentley. In 1913 Bentley reciprocated by dedicating his classic detective novel *Trent's Last Case* to Chesterton. The first of the Father Brown short stories appeared in 1911 and quickly set Chesterton off on a new career as a crime fiction writer to add to his other laurels. He was

Gilbert and Frances outside the studio of their house, Top Meadow, at Beaconsfield.

The Donkey

When fishes flew and forests walked
And figs grew upon thorn,
Some moment when the moon was
    blood
Then surely I was born;
With monstrous head and sickening
    cry
And ears like errant wings,
The devil's walking parody
On all four-footed things.
The tattered outlaw of the earth,
Of ancient crooked will;
Starve, scourge, deride me: I am
    dumb,
I keep my secret still.
Fools! For I also had my hour;
One far fierce hour and sweet:
There was a shout about my ears,
And palms before my feet.

                     G.K.C.

One day the very tall and extremely thin George Bernard Shaw said to Chesterton: *"If I were as fat as you, I'd hang myself."* Chesterton replied: *"If I did decide to hang myself, I'd use you as the rope."*

elected first president of the Detection Club in London, among whose other members were Agatha Christie and Dorothy L. Sayers. In addition he was still writing poetry, producing some of his best. Who can forget his immortal lines:

> *Smile at us, pay us, pass us;*
> *But do not quite forget,*
> *For we are the people of England,*
> *That never has spoken yet.*

This verse, perhaps more than any other he wrote, illustrates his social and political stance — he loathed big business as much as state ownership, advocating instead a

The people of England . . . or quite a number of them, enjoy the sunshine at Bridlington in Yorkshire.

The People of England

by G.K. CHESTERTON

Smile at us, pay us, pass us;
But do not quite forget,
For we are the people of England,
That never has spoken yet.
There is many a fat farmer
That drinks less cheerfully,
There is many a free French peasant
Who is richer and sadder than we.
There are no folk in the whole world
So helpless or so wise.
There is hunger in our bellies,
There is laughter in our eyes;
You laugh at us and love us,
Both mugs and eyes are wet:
Only you do not know us.
For we have not spoken yet.
They have given us into the hand
Of the new unhappy lords,

Lords without anger and honour,
Who dare not carry their swords.
They fight by shuffling papers;
They have bright dead alien eyes;
They look at our labour and laughter
As a tired man looks at flies.
And the load of their loveless pity
Is worse than the ancient wrongs,
Their doors are shut in the evening;
And they know no songs.
We hear men speaking for us
Of new laws strong and sweet,
Yet is there no man speaketh
As we speak in the street.
But we are the people of England;
And we have not spoken yet.
Smile at us, pay us, pass us . . .
But do not quite forget.

G.K. working at his desk in the house at Beaconsfield.

return to cottage industry, small businesses and a property-owning democracy with power vested in the people, not the political manipulators at the top. But such heavy themes were never allowed to dominate his thinking and writing. Humour was never far distant, as evidenced by his wonderfully mobile verse *"The Rolling English Road"*:

Before the Roman came to Rye or out to Severn strode
The rolling English drunkard made the rolling English road . . .

One can just imagine his massive, Billy Bunter type figure cavorting along the higgledy-piggledy track of ancient Saxon lanes, on

That night we went to Birmingham by way of Beachy Head.

The Chestertons had moved to Beaconsfield in 1909, renting a small house known as Overroads, then among fields near the railway station. Later, while sitting in the garden eating gooseberries from a bag, Chesterton looked across the road and pointed at a tree in the middle of a field. He told his wife he would one day like to build a home for them around that tree. By 1912 his writing and lecturing had provided sufficient money for them to buy the field and erect a small studio in it, using the actual tree as a part of its supporting timbers. Ten years later, as their finances improved, the Chestertons built the home of their dreams,

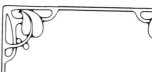

A Romantic in the Rain . . .

The middle classes of modern England are quite fanatically fond of washing; and are often enthusiastic for teetotalism. I cannot therefore comprehend why it is that they exhibit a mysterious dislike of rain. Rain, that inspiring and delightful thing, surely combines the qualities of these two ideals with quite a curious perfection. Our philanthropists are eager to establish public baths everywhere. Rain surely is a public bath; it might almost be called mixed bathing. The appearance of persons coming fresh from this great natural lustration is perhaps not polished or dignified; but for the matter of that, few people are dignified when coming out of a bath. But the scheme of rain in itself is one of enormous purification. It realises the dream of some insane hygienist: it scrubs the sky. Its giant brooms and mops seem to reach the starry rafters and starless corners of the cosmos; it is a cosmic spring-cleaning. If the Englishman is really fond of cold baths, he ought not to grumble at the English climate for being a cold bath. In these days we are constantly told that we should leave our little special possessions and join in the enjoyment of common social institutions and a common social machinery. I offer the rain as a thoroughly Socialist institution. It disregards that degraded delicacy which has hitherto led each gentleman to take his showerbath in private. It is a better showerbath, because it is public and communal; and, best of all, because somebody else pulls the string.   G.K.C.

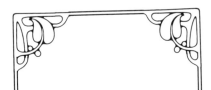

I believe in getting into hot water. I think it keeps you clean.　　　G.K.C.

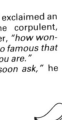

"Oh Mr. Chesterton," exclaimed an ardent admirer of the corpulent, larger than life character, "how wonderful it must be to be so famous that everyone knows who you are."

"If they don't, they soon ask," he replied.

A recent photograph of Top Meadow with a plaque commemorating Chesterton above the door.

"Top Meadow", around the nucleus of that studio, and spent the rest of their lives there.

Chesterton's output continued at an ever-accelerating pace, almost to the day of his death in June 1936. Some 20 years earlier, when his brother Cecil went to France as a soldier, G.K. took over the editorship of his magazine *New Witness*. Cecil died shortly after the Armistice and, despite G.K.'s unstinted efforts, the periodical ended in bankruptcy and closed down in 1923. Two years later Chesterton launched his own publication, *G.K.'s Weekly*, but although it outlived him it never achieved a profit. It

Chesterton's wife, Frances. The absent-minded writer once sent her the following telegram: "Am in Birmingham. Where ought I to be?" She wired back: "Home."

was largely to subsidise its losses that Chesterton would dash off another Father Brown story, selling it to one of the more prosperous London magazines like the *Pall Mall* or *Cassell's*. Later, they appeared in book form and were the bestsellers of their day, eventually being made into motion pictures and, more recently, television plays.

Chesterton's conversion to Rome had long been

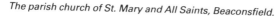

The parish church of St. Mary and All Saints, Beaconsfield.

Merely having an open mind is nothing. The object of opening the mind, as of opening the mouth, is to shut it again on something solid.

G.K.C.

The Main Works of G.K. Chesterton

Greybeards at Play; The Wild Knight (1900); The Defendant (1901); Twelve Types (1902); Robert Browning (1903); The Napoleon of Notting Hill; G.F. Watts (1904); The Club of Queer Trades; Heretics (1905); Charles Dickens (1906); The Man Who Was Thursday; Orthodoxy (1908); George Bernard Shaw; Tremendous Trifles (1909); The Ball and the Cross; What's Wrong with the World?; William Blake (1910); The Innocence of Father Brown; The Ballad of the White Horse (1911); Manalive (1912); The Victorian Age in Literature (1913); The Flying Inn; The Wisdom of Father Brown; The Barbarism of Berlin (1914); The Crimes of England (1915); Lord Kitchener; A Short History of England (1917); Irish Impressions (1919); The Superstition of Divorce (1920); The Ballad of St. Barbara; The Man Who Knew Too Much (1922); Fancies versus Fads; St. Francis of Assisi (1923); The Everlasting Man; William Cobbett (1925); The Incredulity of Father Brown (1926); The Return of Don Quixote; Collected Poems; The Secret of Father Brown; Robert Louis Stevenson (1927); Generally Speaking (1928); The Poet and the Lunatics (1929); The Resurrection of Rome (1930); Chaucer (1932); All I Survey; St. Thomas Aquinas (1933); The Scandal of Father Brown (1935); As I Was Saying (1936). His Autobiography was published post-humously.

The Rolling English Road

BY G.K. CHESTERTON

Before the Roman came to Rye or out to Severn strode,
The rolling English drunkard made the rolling English road.
A reeling road, a rolling road, that rambles round the shire,
And after him the parson ran, the sexton and the squire;
A merry road, a mazy road, and such as we did tread
The night we went to Birmingham by way of Beachy Head.

I knew no harm of Bonaparte and plenty of the Squire,
And for to fight the Frenchman I did not much desire;
But I did bash their baggonets because they came arrayed
To straighten out the crooked road an English drunkard made,
Where you and I went down the lane with ale-mugs in our hands,
The night we went to Glastonbury by way of Goodwin Sands.

His sins they were forgiven him; or why do flowers run
Behind him; and the hedges all strengthening in the sun?
The wild thing went from left to right and knew not which was which,
But the wild rose was above him when they found him in the ditch.
God pardon us, nor harden us; we did not see so clear
The night we went to Bannockburn by way of Brighton Pier.

My friends, we will not go again or ape an ancient rage,
Or stretch the folly of our youth to be the shame of age,
But walk with clearer eyes and ears this path that wandereth,
And see undrugged in evening light the decent inn of death,
For there is good news yet to hear and fine things to be seen,
Before we go to Paradise by way of Kensal Green.

Chesterton the broadcaster. His weekly talks on the BBC during the 1930s were eagerly awaited by listeners and he continued them up to his death in 1936.

The word "good" has many meanings. For example, if a man were to shoot his grandmother at a range of five hundred yards, I should call him a good shot, but not necessarily a good man.
G.K.C.

expected by his close friends, but when it occurred it created a tremendous impact on the public. Hard-line Protestants winced to see one of their intellectual stars return to the ancient Faith, but their dismay was mitigated by the fact that Chesterton's wife remained a staunch Anglican (but only for a further four years). Roman Catholics of the time were naturally jubilant and saw in it a justification of their view that the nearer you get to Truth the closer you get to Rome. The ripples of controversy over Chesterton's conversion spread far and wide — today, happily, such a move would hardly merit a mention in the Press because true Christianity is at last surfacing above the sea of denominational strife. However, old prejudices and deep-rooted bigotry die hard, as witness Northern Ireland, but change is coming, though it may take generations to permeate through all levels of society. No one religion will be the victor — only truth, and pearl-wisdomed Christianity. For the last commandment left by Christ himself was that we should "love one another as I have loved you".

G.K. Chesterton tried to do just that.

G.K Chesterton's grave in Beaconsfield churchyard.

ROMANY OF THE BBC

(1884-1943)

The gypsy broadcaster who brought the countryside into millions of homes

Back in the dark and weary days of the last war, when many English children spent countless hours indoors, or were confined for long stretches to a bunk in an air-raid shelter, the gloom of it all was lifted for half an hour once a week by the calming sound of a man and his dog rambling about in the countryside, striding through lark-filled meadows and across gurgling streams.

Somehow his genial manner, and his deep, soothing voice, transported the youngsters listening to the BBC's "Children's Hour" from the grimness of their wartime reality to the wonder of an England at peace, where birds and animals, brooks and fields awaited the young country walker.

And the man who worked this weekly miracle was known to them all affectionately as "Romany" who, with his barking dog Raq and the two girlish voices of his companions, Doris and Muriel, delighted millions of listeners with broadcasts which seemingly came from either the depths of the countryside, inside his gypsy caravan, or by the campfire in a rural glade. In ten golden years, from 1933 to 1943, he became the most popular of all children's broadcasters and when he died, suddenly, aged 59, the announcement on the six o'clock news that night shocked children everywhere and caused the BBC's switchboard to be jammed with calls from distracted parents unable to console their weeping youngsters. And not only the young mourned his passing — soldiers, sailors, airmen, politicians and professors, all confessed to a love for his programme . . . "Out with Romany".

Such was the magic of the man that millions knew as

Romany, the popular children's broadcaster and country writer, with his English cocker
spaniel, Raq. The picure captured Romany's life and character perfectly and was his own
personal favourite.

The sun was shining in all its glory as Tim, Raq and I set out. The air was balmy, and the hawthorn buds on the hedges were eager to open. Everywhere birds were singing. The woods rang with the falling cadence of the willow warblers; chaffinches "pinked", wrens rattled their alarms at our approach, and far above us the larks sprayed their territories with challenging music.

from Out with Romany Again

A rare photograph of the young Romany with his evangelist parents, George and Tilly Evens.

Romany, but who was in real life an ordained Methodist minister, the Reverend George Bramwell Evens.

Romany's love of the countryside was probably inherited, for his mother, Tilly, was the sister of "Gypsy" Smith — otherwise known as Captain Rodney Smith of the Salvation Army. Both were of full-blooded gypsy stock and were born in a horse-drawn caravan. Later the whole family became converted to the Christian cause. While stationed in Hull, Tilly fell in love with a handsome Salvationist officer from Plymouth, Lieutenant George Evens, and a year after their wedding in 1883 their only son, Bramwell, was born. Tilly and her gorgio husband (i.e. a non-gypsy) later left the Salvation Army and became

20

roving evangelists, taking young Bramwell with them to many parts of northern England where they held revival meetings. Sometimes Bramwell joined them on the platform, for even at the tender age of four he was able to capture an audience's heart with the sweetness of his singing. Eventually his parents settled in Liverpool, where Bramwell's father was appointed missioner at the Wesleyan Church in Cranmer Street. But the little lad was given a difficult time at school where his half-gypsy origin brought him the derision of other pupils. One contemporary belief at the time was that gypsies kidnapped children, and this led to much taunting.

One of the teachers at Aspden Grove School, Lodge Lane, Liverpool, nicknamed young Bramwell "Black Eyes" and the description was quite apt for his dark eyes were a striking feature of his appearance and a sure pointer to his ancestral origins.

Although he continued to assist his parents in their missionary work, he also found time to spend many hours walking in the countryside, with his dog, or staying at home playing with his other pets — white mice, pigeons and rabbits. At 13 his parents sent him to boarding school — Epworth College, Rhyl — where he enjoyed four happy years. Summer holidays were spent on a farm, where Bramwell developed his love for animals and all forms of Nature.

When as a young man he decided to enter the Methodist ministry he spent 18 months at Queen's College, Taunton, and later a year at Colchester as a probationer on the circuit, allowing him much time to explore the wonders of the Essex marshes and countryside.

After a spell at the Wesleyan Theological College at Handsworth, Birmingham, he was ordained in 1908 and despite his yearning for the countryside was sent to a shabby city circuit at Dalston, east London. But there were two great consolations — his proximity to Epping Forest, which afforded him an outlet for his Nature-loving instincts, and the chance meeting with a pretty girl from a neighbouring Congregational church, Eunice Thomas, who became his bride in 1910. Following his duties in London he was sent to Goole in Yorkshire, but it was his next posting to Carlisle in 1914 that brought him his greatest delight, for walking in the Cumberland fells, fishing in the Eden, or marvelling at the beauties of the Lakes were to have a lasting influence on his life.

Young Bramwell Evens with his first dog, Floss. As a boy he captivated many people with his sweet singing voice.

Two partridges ran into the shelter of the hedge as Comma turned a bend in the lane, and Raq left his seat on the driving-board to follow them with his usual optimism into the field on our right. A spaniel never gives up hoping that his quarry will die of heart-failure if he only chases it long enough!

from *Out With Romany Again*

21

The old town hall opposite the cross in Carlisle. Romany was posted to the Cumberland town in 1914.

It was in Carlisle that his attempts to join the Colours was thwarted, for Army doctors discovered that he had a "murmuring heart". So he turned instead to literature and, drawing on the many friendships he had made among rural folk, and the experience of their ways, he began writing about country matters as well as preaching the word of God in his church — the Central Hall at Carlisle, which he built during his ministry there.

In 1921, while attending the Appleby horse fair he persuaded a gypsy to sell him a caravan — called a "vardo" in Romany language which he spoke — for £75. He then hired a horse and drove it back to the Methodist manse at Carlisle . . . later it was to play a large part in his broadcasting and books.

After spending many holidays and weekends in their caravan in the lush Cumberland countryside, the Reverend Bramwell Evens and his family — they now had two children, a boy (Glyn) and a daughter called Romany June — were moved to Huddersfield and then in 1929 to Halifax. All the time he was writing, and his Nature column appeared in many newspapers under the pen-name of "The Tramp".

While at Halifax he began considering leaving the ministry because of his heart problems, and series of headaches, and perhaps the idea of becoming a professional writer crossed his mind. He had developed the ability to sketch, and in his talks to children he used a chalk and blackboard to illustrate his stories of wild life. He was also very interested in photography. All these talents were yet to be brought together, however, when he started writing a

Many people say that the weasel mesmerises the rabbit. But, personally, I don't believe it. I think the rabbit mesmerises itself. I think I told you before that if it had the sense to run as fast as ever it could in one direction, it would have a chance of escaping. But, instead of doing that, it loses its head when it knows the weasel is on its trail, and wastes time by stopping to listen, or by running aimlessly in circles. It keeps saying to itself: 'I can't get away — I can't get away,' and finally it lies down and lets itself be killed without trying to resist.

from Out With Romany Again

22

weekly nature column for the *Huddersfield Examiner*. By writing about his friends, country arts and crafts, nature lore, and so on, Bramwell struck a vein of literary gold and inevitably he began to receive invitations not to preach so much as to expand on his articles. Not that he would have seen much difference between the two, for his was a theology of Nature, with God not confined to heaven, but at work in the beauty of the world. His growing fame was not resented by the kindly folk of Halifax. Indeed, his appreciative congregation found him a fine manse in Rothwell Road, permitting him to extend his writing activities.

Bramwell was never conventional, and tales abound as to his appearance when on an excursion into the country-side. It was not for nothing that he originally called himself "The Tramp". Some people might have expected their minister to look thoroughly respectable even in his leisure time, but no-one was surprised to see him in his old clothes, darting across a field. The children adored him, naturally, and to the end of his days his home was "open house" for youngsters seeking advice on their pets.

In 1933, after meeting an acquaintance in the street at Manchester who suggested he ought to audition for the BBC's "Children's Hour", he was asked under what name he would be known — for it was the fashion in those days for children's broadcasters to be called Uncle this or Auntie that. But "Uncle Bramwell"? — or the Reverend Evens? On the spur of the moment, and perhaps recalling his own gypsy origins and the name of his daughter, he said "Romany" . . . and from then on, to everyone in radio and to the vast listening audience, it became his only name.

So began the ten happiest years of his life. The broadcasts used to go out between 5.30 and 6pm, on Friday evenings to begin with when only the North of England could receive his programme. But later when it was broadcast throughout all the regions it was switched to Tuesday.

Romany — a dusky-skinned six-footer with jet-black hair combed sharply back from a deep forehead — would settle into a chair in the studio, with Raq the spaniel at his side . . . then the signature tune faded (the haunting melody titled "Lullaby of the Leaves") and the announcer said simply: "And now, children, we are going . . . Out with Romany . . ."

Youngsters in city slums discovered, through this gentle countryman, how to identify birds by their different

Romany in his "dog collar", with his wife Eunice in 1930.

Romany's "vardo" which he bought from a gypsy in 1921 for £75. Today the caravan stands in a small garden sanctuary near the Public Library at Wilmslow, Cheshire.

"How good a pipe tastes on a morning like this," I said to Raq. I was sitting contentedly on the stile near the vardo, enjoying the luxury of being thoroughly lazy. Raq sniffed at the pipe and then drew back his head in disgust. The look he gave me as he licked his nose suggested that I had played a trick on him.

I sat and watched the yellow bees sweeping from one flower to another. The heavy bumble bees, too, were industriously collecting pollen — like stout market women weighed down with their purchases. And the way in which their buzzing note took on a deeper tone when two of them met in mid-air — as though exchanging morning courtesies — lent colour to my fancy.

from *Out With Romany Again*

songs, and were encouraged to keep pets and be kind to all animals. Others learnt to look for hedgehogs beneath piles of dead leaves, to discover — without disturbing — birds' nests, or to listen for the plop of a vole under a river bank. Schools throughout the country used Romany's rambles on which to base their Nature lessons, and encouraged their pupils to read his books. In addition to the estimated four million children who tuned in to his broadcasts, another nine million adults listened regularly . . . for at a turbulent and anxious time in our history Romany's gentle chats and unhurried style smoothed the furrows from the nation's brow. His programme provided a much-needed medicine for tortured minds.

Combining sound effects with narrative in an amazingly effective way, considering the primitive nature of recording apparatus in those days, the programmes came across as real excursions into the fields and meadows, by streams and rivers. When after Romany's death a rather pointless article in the *Radio Times* revealed that the programmes had all been made in the studio, few listeners believed it. They felt that they had been really "Out with Romany" in the countryside.

His two "young" friends, Muriel and Doris, were included in the programmes, and later featured in the many books he wrote. But perhaps the most popular character of all was Raq. He appeared in public, too. When Romany spoke to schools, or other groups of children, he would pause during his address and ask, "Do you want to see Raq?" As the children roared their reply, the dog was let loose from a side room. He would bound onto the stage and, with tail wagging, would leap into Romany's arms.

The researcher into periodicals of the 1930s is soon impressed by the amount of work achieved by this remarkable man. In her enjoyable biography *Through the Years With Romany* (University of London Press, 1946) his widow, Eunice Evens, probably underrates his ability, certainly as evidenced by his earlier work, when she writes: "He knew that it was not his literary ability that induced the various newspaper editors to ask him to contribute to their columns, even before he made a reputation as Romany. It was his unusual knowledge of the happenings in the countryside week by week, and the humour and pathos with which he interpreted them . . . for 17 years, he wrote 2,000 words weekly to the *Cumberland News*, and his column of the same length to the *Methodist Recorder* lasted for 23 years. His contributions to the *Yorkshire Post* and *Huddersfield Examiner* continued for 6 and 14 years respectively, and over a period of 25 years he must have written several million words." The stories in *The Sunday Circle*, a popular Christian weekly, published during 1934, show a fine mastery of dialect, and a wry humour that would certainly be appreciated by country-starved readers today.

In 1939, Romany retired from the ministry and he and his wife moved to Wilmslow, Cheshire. The move had been planned several months earlier, so that he could be in easy reach of the BBC studios at Manchester, from where he made his broadcasts. Theoretically, he was also anticipating retirement from lecturing, too, though as he was still speaking to groups all over the country, this well-deserved rest seemed far in the distance. Now that war had come, Romany became involved in helping the morale of children — for his talks on the enduring ways of Nature seemed a powerful antidote to the threats of invasion and bombing.

In her biography, Eunice Evens wrote of her husband's church work thus: "He was no scholar; he did not delve deeply into theology, nor attempt to explain many of the more intricate mysteries of the Christian faith, some of

"When you get fed up with present-day happenings, go out into the lanes and the fields, and listen and look at the things of Nature. There is no hurry in that world — that is why I am a dodderer. I lose all sense of time when I'm in the country, forget the speed of machinery . . . To be a dodderer is a lost art these days, one that we should recapture."

— from a talk by Romany, 1941

which he frankly owned he did not understand himself. In simple language he would state what he himself believed, and was inclined rather to try to rid religion of the man-made ritualistic incrustations of the centuries, and present the life of Christ in its simplicity and beauty.

"He had no voice specially reserved for pulpit utterances, as so many preachers have; whether he was reading the Scriptures or praying, it was the same unaffected voice that afterwards became so loved.

"He loved the poetry of the Psalms, and he made the dramatic stories of the Old Testament live. Religion to him was a very practical thing, for he had little mysticism about him. He would tell us that holiness was not some vague, nebulous virtue, but wholeness, and that being holy meant that one served God and one's fellow-men not only with one's emotions, but with one's mind and with one's bodily energy.

"His pulpit attitude towards life was usually one of optimism and thankfulness, and his sermons and prayers were veined with gratitude for being alive, for the quiet, simple things of life, the treasures of the world of nature, the wealth of friendships, the joy experienced in helping others, all of which, he would tell his congregation, were to be had without money and without price."

Romany died on 20th November, 1943. After several hours spent digging in the garden he came in for a rest. Half an hour after lying down, his wife found he had passed on . . . making his exit from life as he made his walks from one field to another, with hardly a sound.

The news of his death was broadcast on both the six o'clock and nine o'clock news that night and the BBC switchboard was inundated with callers. Hundreds of letters poured in from young listeners worried about Raq, thinking he would now be left alone in the caravan. But not only the children of war-torn England felt the loss of Romany. So too did his wider audience, from the men in uniform, those at sea, even University dons and stalwart

The house in Wilmslow, Cheshire, to where Romany and his wife moved in 1939. He died there in 1943.

26

For all his popularity and contact with "modern" broadcasting, like any gypsy, Romany was always happiest when he was out in the countryside by his own camp fire.

policemen . . . everyone, it seemed, who loved the English countryside would miss his Tuesday night rambles with Muriel, Doris and Raq.

But his old caravan is still there in a small public garden, dedicated to Romany, near the Library at Wilmslow, displaying poems sent in by children upon his death. There are other memorials to him in various parts, including a wall tablet at an Ilford animal clinic.

But perhaps his greatest tribute of all remains in the memory of those people today who still recall the half-hour of happiness he provided — so simple and straightforward, so unvulgar and unvain — as he escorted us on those childhood-echoing rambles . . . "Out with Romany".

Farewell to Romany

Goodbye, dear friend. If we no more
   shall roam
Fresh woods with you, nor fields
   your voice made cool;
Nor find the fieldmouse in his harvest
   home,
The brown trout in the pool;

Nor with hands made more gentle at
   your words,
Pick up the shrew mouse or the
   trembling hare;
Nor, with ears wiser, name the
   singing birds
In trees no longer bare.

If we no more with you shall do these
   things,
Let us, at least, say sometimes when
   the clear
Spring skies are full of song and
   woods with wings,
"I wish that he was here."

Then shall we keep your memory
   green and true;
Then shall the lovely world more
   lovely grow,
And you, dear Romany, I think
   that you
Would wish to have it so.

       GEOFFREY DEARMER

This poem was read at the BBC Memorial Broadcast for Romany in 1944.

MARY WEBB

(1881-1927)

The Shropshire lass whose life was touched by tragedy

The Vision

In the busy tongues of Spring
There's an angel carolling.
Kneeling low in any place,
We may see the Father's face;
Standing quiet anywhere,
Hear our Lady speaking fair;
And in daily marketings
Feel the rush of beating wings.
Watching always, wonderingly,
All the faces passing by,
There we see through pain and wrong
Christ look out, serene and strong.

M.W.

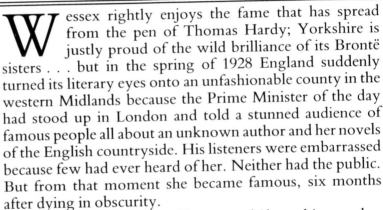

Wessex rightly enjoys the fame that has spread from the pen of Thomas Hardy; Yorkshire is justly proud of the wild brilliance of its Brontë sisters . . . but in the spring of 1928 England suddenly turned its literary eyes onto an unfashionable county in the western Midlands because the Prime Minister of the day had stood up in London and told a stunned audience of famous people all about an unknown author and her novels of the English countryside. His listeners were embarrassed because few had ever heard of her. Neither had the public. But from that moment she became famous, six months after dying in obscurity.

Her name was Mary Webb . . . and Shropshire was her world.

Most strangers to the hilly county on the Welsh border might connect it, at least in literature, with the brilliant A.E. Housman for his classic verse *"A Shropshire Lad"*. But Housman was a native of Worcestershire, and admitted that apart from Ludlow and Wenlock he did not know the Shropshire countryside very well. Mary Webb, however, had sprung from its soil, and in later years G.K. Chesterton was to hail her as "The Shropshire Lass".

She was born Mary Gladys Meredith, at Leighton Lodge, twelve miles south east of Shrewsbury, on 25th March, 1881 — rather fittingly it was Lady Day, and the first day of the spring quarter. As her personal and literary life was later to prove, the pull of Nature — and spring in particular — was to be one of the strongest influences of her talented but troubled life. She was the first of six children, and came from strong middle-class stock. Her father, George Edward Meredith, was an Oxford Master of Arts

*Mary Webb, the Shropshire novelist and poet, photographed in 1925
just two years before her death.*

Mary at the age of 15. She enjoyed long walks in the Shropshire country-side with her father who told her stories about local legends and superstitions.

The Pool

Secretly, under the heavy rho-dodendron leaves and in the furtive silence beneath the yew-trees, gnats danced. Their faint motions made the garden stiller; their smallness made it oppressive; their momentary life made it infinitely old. Then Undern Pool was full of leaf shadows like multitudinous lolling tongues, and the smell of the mud tainted the air — half sickly, half sweet. The clipped bushes and the twisted chimneys made inky shadows like steeples on the grass, and great trees of rose, beautiful in desolation, drip-ped with red and white and elbowed the guelder roses and the elders set with white patens.

M.W. from *Gone to Earth*

graduating in Classics, and kept a small prep school for boys at his home. He was a cultured religious man with a deep sense of piety, and his well-remembered kindnesses among the local poor were matched only by his rich sense of humour and deeply sympathetic nature. In 1880, when aged 40, he married Sarah Alice Scott, the 29-year-old daughter of an Edinburgh doctor who claimed kinship with Sir Walter Scott, and brought his bride to live in his native Shropshire. Although Mary resembled her mother in stature, she inherited her father's deep love of Nature and poetry . . . and his almost legendary unselfishness.

Mary's birthplace was an idyllic spot, close to the mys-terious Wrekin, the 1,330ft hill which has always sym-bolised Shropshire . . . but when yet a baby her parents moved to the Grange, a lovely English country house near Much Wenlock, an old town that has changed little since Mary's childhood. She spent the most formative years of her life here, from 1882-1896, and her father often took her for long walks or pony trap rides along the winding tracks of nearby Wenlock Edge, the magnificent 20-mile-long spine of Shropshire. It was in this lush countryside that Mary learned from her father the legends and superstitions associated with her county. He called her his "precious bane", quoting from Milton's *Paradise Lost*. The nick-name was to have particular significance later on.

One of these old stories was the tale of "The Major's Leap" — now the name of a sheer cliff face forming part of Wenlock Edge, and still popular among visitors to Shrop-shire's inner heart today. During the Civil War a Shrop-shire cavalier, Major Smallwood, escaped a posse of pursu-ing Roundheads by galloping his horse over the edge of the sheer drop. Mount and rider landed among trees and although the horse died, the major survived. His feat lived on in Mary's imagination, evoking pity and passion in her tender heart — pity for the man hunted down like a fox; passion, and a growing revulsion, against blood sports in which her parents, and most of her friends, took part as members of the local fox-hunt.

Later, this early stirring of deep feeling against all forms of cruelty and suffering was to manifest itself in her second novel *Gone to Earth* which told of a Shropshire girl and her pet fox, pursued by hounds and huntsmen, who hurled herself — still clutching the animal — over the edge of a quarry to escape, albeit in death. In 1895 Mary's mother fell from her horse while taking part in a hunt, suffering from

Much Wenlock, the little town that has hardly changed at all since the days when Mary and her parents attended church there.

To Life

*Fair, fierce Life! What will you do
    with me?
What will you make me?
Take me and break me,
Hurt me or love me,
But throne me not lonely and safely
    above thee
Sweet Life!*

M.W.

Market Day

Early there come travelling
    On market day,
Old men and young men
    From far away,
With red fruits of the orchard
    And dark fruits of the hill,
Dew-fresh garden stuff
    And mushrooms chill,
Honey from the brown skep,
    Brown eggs, and posies
Of gillyflowers and Lent lilies
    And blush roses . . .

M.W.

spinal injury which kept her confined to her bedroom for five years, and making Mary — the eldest daughter — something of a little mother to her younger brothers and sisters. It was at this time that the Meredith household was increased by the arrival of a governess, Miss Edith Lory, who displayed firm kindliness and great commonsense in tutoring all six children. Of Mary she later wrote:

I saw at once she had a very sweet nature, and next to her father whom she adored, she was the most unselfish of a fine-natured household. She was devoted to her younger brothers and sisters, and her care of them gave her an old-fashioned motherly way as a girl. I helped her with her studies for the next four years. She was always ready to learn.

When 14, Mary was sent to a finishing school for girls at Southport, the resort on Lancashire's flat coastline and far away from her native Shropshire hills. During this period the Merediths moved again, this time to the Woodlands at Stanton-upon-Hine Heath, north of Shrewsbury, the county town, and cynically said to be "five miles from any-where". At 16 Mary returned from Southport to help the governess teach the little Merediths, and to take an active part in running the household, as her mother was still confined to her bedroom.

Gradually Mary blossomed into an attractive young

The Market Place, Shrewsbury.

The Secret Joy

Face to face with the sunflower,
Cheek to cheek with the rose,
We follow a secret highway
Hardly a traveller knows.
The gold that lies in the folded
      bloom
Is all our wealth;
We eat of the heart of the forest
With innocent stealth.
We know the ancient roads
In the leaf of a nettle,
And bathe in the blue profound
Of a speedwell petal.

M.W.

Walkers enjoy a picnic beside the brooding waters of a tarn on Shropshire's mysterious Long Mynd.

woman. Although only 5ft 2ins, she was slim with long dark hair coiled in a bun. When in her early twenties, she would sometimes leave home for up to a fortnight, taking pens and paper, and go away to the depths of the Shropshire countryside, quite unchaperoned, to write poetry in the "lost and forgotten places" of hill and mere. It was on these sorties that she imbibed the depth of feeling for everything of Nature. She knew every kind of bird, tree, and plant by sight — even able to discern the different wild flowers by their scent. Often she would lie in the dew-wet grasses of the fields at dawn to watch the petals of daisies unfold to the sun.

Mary first began writing poetry as a young girl, and her work always had merit. Later, while living at Stanton, she began writing short articles for the parish magazine, and then helped deliver copies to houses in the area, often visiting cottages of the poor with whom she quickly developed a strong bond of affection, despite her natural shyness which was to remain with her for life. At 20 she was first struck down with a thyroid illness — Graves' Disease — for which there was no cure at the time. Through the summer of 1901 she lay critically ill in bed, and when she did recover her appearance was markedly affected by a goitre in the base of her neck, deathly pale skin, excessive thinness, and large protruding eyes.

She considered herself ugly, wore high-necked blouses

A corner of old Shrewsbury, the market town of Shropshire.

to hide the swollen neck, and shut herself away as much as possible from people outside the family circle, sensitive to the curious glances of strangers. During her slow convalescence she began writing essays, nine of which were eventually to be published under the title *The Spring of Joy*, which illustrated her close involvement with Nature. Before she had made a complete recovery her parents had moved yet again — this time to a lovely old mill house in the village of Meole Brace, on the outskirts of Shrewsbury. Mary loved this old town with its gabled houses, narrow winding streets and depth of history.

Gradually recovering her strength, Mary continued to live the life of a recluse, protected still by her father's love . . . until his death, in the bitter January of 1909, after

Music

"I hope, Edward," said Mrs. Marston, "that it won't be serious music. I think serious music interferes with the digestion. Your poor father and I went to the *Creation* on our honeymoon, and thought little of it; then we went to the *Crucifixion*, and though it was very pleasant, I couldn't digest the oysters afterwards. And then, again, these clever musicians allow themselves to become so passionate, one almost thinks they are inebriated. Not flutes and cornets, they have to think of their breath, but fiddlers can wreak their feelings on instruments without suffering for it."

M.W. from *Gone to Earth*

Mary Webb in 1920 when she was aged 39.

Green Rain

Into the scented woods we'll go
And see the blackthorn swim in snow.
High above, in the budding leaves,
A brooding dove awakes and grieves;
The glades with mingled music stir,
And wildly laughs the woodpecker.
When blackthorn petals pearl the
    breeze,
There are the twisted hawthorn trees
Thick-set with buds, as clear and pale
As golden water or green hail —
As if a storm of rain had stood
Enchanted in the thorny wood,
And, hearing fairy voices call,
Hung poised, forgetting how to fall.

M.W.

falling from a ladder. Mary sat by his bedside through the crisis, embroidering quietly as his life ebbed away. She later penned her thoughts:

On that last night, embroidering by his bed,
I often paused, his loving smile to meet,
And hear the tender approving words he said:
'Your work is very beautiful, my sweet!'
The embroidery stays unfinished: Life's design
Must yet be stitched. How can I raise my head —
And no smile there? Lest sudden tears of mine
Should stain the cloth, and dull the silver thread.

Mary's intense grief affected her health for years to come, and she never recovered properly from the pang caused by his death, but her suffering motivated her writing skills still further, and it was from the agony of this spiritual wilderness that she formed the basis of her first novel *The Golden Arrow*, although it was not written until five years later. In the summer of 1909 she sent a short story to *Country Life* and it was accepted — a signal success. But a more significant event took place a few months later when a schoolteacher — Henry Bertram Law Webb — came to live in Meole Brace. He was a Cambridge graduate, fluent in seven languages, and nephew of Captain Matthew Webb who achieved world fame in 1875 as the first man to swim the English Channel, only to meet a tragic death eight years later at Niagara Falls, Canada.

Henry met Mary — almost five years his senior — at a local literary gathering and since both were writers concerned with the philosophy of Nature their attraction was mutual and immediate. Together they explored the hills and lanes of their beloved Shropshire, and in 1911 Henry's book of essays *The Silences of the Moon* was published. A year later the handsome and eligible bachelor of 26 married the shy, nervous spinster in the village church — and, typical of Mary, her invited guests were the women inmates of the local workhouse! Such was her love of the poor and complete lack of class-consciousness. She dressed her only bridesmaid — the three-year-old daughter of her family's gardener — in a new white dress of *broderie anglaise* — but Mary herself, in the fashion of poorer country girls at that time, and as a mark of her own simplicity, wore plain muslin.

After her marriage Mary went to live in the Somerset resort of Weston-super-Mare, where her husband took up a teaching post, but after two restless years away from her beloved Shropshire the couple returned in 1914. They

34

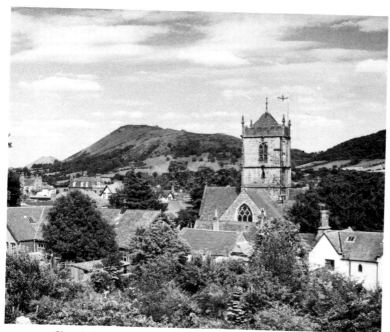

Church Stretton, the "Shepwardine" of Mary Webb's novels.

rented an isolated house — Rose Cottage, at Pontesbury, nine miles south west of Shrewsbury — and planned to live on Mary's annual allowance of £100 from the Scott family trust, and the proceeds of their own writings. The cottage was at the foot of Pontesford Hill, part of the range of hills which includes The Long Mynd.

Here, they spent the happiest years of their life together, writing and working in the large garden. Henry had been turned down for army service, due to a back injury, and Mary did most of the digging. As food prices soared, due to the war, Mary's fruit and vegetable produce became more vital to their cottage economy. She regularly gave food to old folk in the area, and any tramp or beggar who passed by. Even so, she had a surplus and rented a stall on Shrewsbury Market, selling her fruit, flowers and green-grocery at prices well below other stall-holders . . .yet another indication of her feeling for the hardships of others, even though she herself was short of money.

Often she would rise hours before dawn and walk with her bundles of produce the nine miles to Shrewsbury on market day (Saturday) and the same distance back again at night. Henry stayed at home, but occasionally wheeled a barrow of fruit to sell cheaply to villagers.

This experience helped her write her first novel, *The*

Mary dedicated the following poem which she wrote shortly after his death in 1909, to her father George Edward Meredith (pictured below).

Treasures

These are my treasures: just a word, a look,
A chiming sentence from his favourite book,
A large, blue, scented blossom that he found
And plucked for me in some enchanted ground,
A joy he planned for us, a verse he made
Upon a birthday, the increasing shade
Of trees he planted by the waterside,
The echo of a laugh, his tender pride
In those he loved, his hand upon my hair,
The dear voice lifted in his evening prayer.

How safe they must be kept! So dear, so few,
And all I have to last my whole life through.
A silver mesh of loving words entwining,
At every crossing thread a tear-drop shining,
Shall close them in. Yet since my tears may break
The slender thread of brittle words, I'll make
A safer, humbler hiding-place apart,
And lock them in the fastness of my heart.

M.W.

The past is only the present become invisible and mute...We are tomorrow's past. Even now we slip away...we, that were the new thing, gather magic as we go.

M.W. from *Precious Bane*

A view over the rooftops of Ludlow which appears in Precious Bane *as the market town of Lullingford.*

Golden Arrow, published in 1916, which is rich in Shropshire dialect and old customs. It was also to be useful as background for what is probably the most famous of her books — *Precious Bane*, published in 1924 — in which the main character Prudence Sarn, a country girl with a hare lip, walks many miles to sell her wares in the market at Lullingford, based on the ancient town of Ludlow in the south of the county.

In 1916 Mary and Henry, finding it hard to make ends meet, moved again — this time to a lonely and isolated hill cottage called "The Nills", hidden under the remote northern slopes of the Stiperstones range. Henry took up a teaching post in Chester, where they lived during the week with Mary's widowed mother, returning to the Shropshire cottage at weekends — its rental was only £13 a year. But Chester itself, or more likely the enforced exile from Shropshire, depressed Mary and after only one term Henry resigned and secured a teaching position in Shrewsbury, which is the Silverton of her novels.

In 1917 the couple bought a piece of land on the thickly-wooded crest of Lyth Hill and, with a bank mortgage of £250, had a small house built — Spring Cottage. Here at last was the home that Mary had always longed for, and they moved in as her second novel *Gone to Earth* was

Broadgate in Ludlow.

36

Ramblers cross the barren Stiperstones, a range of hills which plays an important part in Mary Webb's novel The Golden Arrow.

Echoes

... we are as full of echoes as a rocky wood — echoes of the past, reflex echoes of the future, and echoes of the soil ... The echoes are in us of great voices long gone hence, the unknown cries of huge beasts on the mountains; the sullen aims of creatures in the slime; the lovecall of the bittern ... the ceremonial that passes yearly in the emerald temples of bud and calyx — we have walked those temples; we are the sacrifice on those altars. And the future floats on the current of our blood like a secret argosy.

M.W. from *Gone to Earth*

published. She would spend hours on end outside in the open air, in all weathers and regardless of her health, noting every detail of Nature's changing scene, and writing down her tumbling thoughts. She would often spend whole days in the woods, deep in meditation.

Mary's life-style now classed her as an eccentric, and she would often be seen in an old coat and faded gown, striding through fields with sopping wet shoes and muddy skirts. But her writings were becoming more appreciated by the famous few including Walter de la Mare and John Buchan. Rebecca West claimed *Gone to Earth* was "the novel of the year" and declared "Mary Webb is a genius". Even so, the public did not respond and sales of her books were poor, throwing yet another strain on the Webbs' slender fortunes.

Later that year she began working on yet another novel which some critics consider her best — *The House in Dormer Forest*, eventually published in 1920; in it she reflects on her own childlessness through the character of Amber Darke, a spinster whose love for the strong and silent Michael Hallowes mirrors her own relationship with her husband. Although Mary yearned for a baby, this joy was to be denied her, and she poured out her maternal love on the poor children of the neighbourhood, and those she found in the back streets of Shrewsbury. She bought whole outfits of clothes, shoes and food for the street waifs whom

John Buchan, author of The Thirty-Nine Steps, *who was one of several prominent writers to praise Mary Webb's work.*

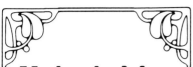

Under the Moon

After a while I came to a great gnarled hawthorn hedge... Within its precincts dwelt intense sweetness; and there I stayed, looking into the next field through an interstice of the twisty branches. The young rabbits were out under the moon, wild with excitement, the very soul of gaiety: they were washing their faces, dashing off at a tangent, leaping over lakes of pale light. Parents, grandparents, and great-grandparents were there, frisking with abandon in the athletic manner of Dickens's old folk at Christmas. Off went a stripling, bounding over a lake, landing in the middle, dashing away with a delighted kick, as if he said — "Ha! Only moonshine water!" A grandfather, watching as he trimmed his whiskers, was fired to do likewise, gleefully beating the record.

What is that stir in the grass at the root of the thorn? A grave hedgehog slips out and watches in a superior manner. Suddenly she becomes infected with the revelry, and rushes away at a surprising pace to share the general energy of enjoyment. Behind her come four minute hedgehogs, replicas of their mother, except that their spines are nearly white and their ears hang down. Like her, they run in the manner of toy animals upon invisible wheels. They all go at a speed one could not have believed possible, joining in the fun, recklessly negotiating the fairy rings; and their absurd little shadows follow madly after.

M.W. from *The Spring of Joy*

Spring Cottage on Lyth Hill, the home for which Mary had always longed.

she found begging, and recorded them forever in her beautiful poem *"To a Little Child Begging"* . . .

> Poor little traveller, lost in night!
> God made a miracle, I know,
> To give you life — tears and delight,
> And ecstasy and ancient woe.
> Yet barefoot in the snow you stand,
> Beseeching bread with shaking hand.
> Poor baby, with your wistful face!
> When you are grown a man, and tall,
> You'll have the kingly, simple grace,
> The smile that makes a festival.
> Yet from the dark your hungry eyes
> Behold the cook-shop's paradise.

She spent her advance royalties on gifts for local people, and on one occasion even bought a piano for a child who expressed a desire to learn music. At Christmas every child living on Lyth Hill received a gift . . . but her largesse sometimes caused resentment, and comparisons were inevitably made by local mothers.

Partly due to Mary's growing literary output, the Webbs moved to London in 1921 where Henry secured a teaching position at Golders Green, but they retained the cottage on Lyth Hill for occasional visits. While here, in October 1922, her fourth novel *Seven For a Secret* was published . . . but London drained Mary of happiness, and she found herself immersed in a sea of sophisticated callousness as city-based authors sought to belittle the drab little woman from the hills of Shropshire. Yet others sprang to her aid — Edwin Pugh, writing in the *Bookman*, declared:

"To pass from the work of the average modern novelist to the work of Mary Webb is like stepping out of a stuffy room into the fresh air".

In 1923 she began writing *Precious Bane*, while living in Grove Cottages, Hampstead, and shortly after her mother's death in April of the following year it was published . . . but little more than a thousand copies were sold in the first year. The lack of success, and its consequent financial pressure, caused Mary's health to deteriorate yet again. She found herself at frequent odds with her husband who preferred staying at school long into the evening, often tutoring boys and girls for further exams, rather than returning home to an increasingly distraught wife surrounded by household debts.

It was then that Mary would return, sad and alone, to Spring Cottage to find solace from affliction and heartache in the bosom of her beloved Shropshire. In the summer of 1926 Mary was awarded the Femina Vie Heureuse prize for *Precious Bane* — a coveted literary award for "the best imaginative work in prose or verse descriptive of English life by an author who has not gained sufficient recogniton". But still financial success evaded her.

As the new year dawned, and Mary began writing what was to be her last novel, she received the greatest praise of all, from an unexpected source — a letter from 10 Downing Street, personally written by the Prime Minister, Stanley Baldwin.

He had read *Precious Bane* during the Christmas holiday and was so taken with it that he felt compelled to write to the author, in January 1927:

Dear Mrs. Webb,

I hope you will not think it an impertinence on my part if I tell you with what keen delight I have read 'Precious Bane'.

My people lived in Shropshire for centuries before they migrated to Worcestershire, and I spent my earliest years in Bewdley which is on the border. In your book I seem to hear again the speech and turns of phrase which surrounded me in the nursery. I think it is a really first-class piece of work and I have not enjoyed a book so much for years.

It was given to me by one of my secretaries and I read it at Christmas within sight of the Clee Hills, at home.

Thank you a thousand times for it.

    Believe me to remain
      Sincerely yours,
        Stanley Baldwin

The Snowdrop

Three softly curved white petals
    veined with light,
Three green-lined sepals, guarding
    frugal gold,
And all so strong to fold or unfold!
Snow thunders from the bending
    pines. How slight
This frail, sheathed stem! Yet all
    unbent it springs,
So swift in stoopings and recoverings.
In the pale sunshine, with frail wings
    unfurled,
Comes to the bending snowdrop the
    first bee.
She gives her winter honey prudently;
And faint with travel in a bitter world,
The bee makes music, tentative and
    low,
And Spring awakes and laughs across
    the snow.

                M.W.

The Grange, Wenlock Edge.

MARY WEBB WALK

(about seven miles)

1. From Much Wenlock (Priory, 16th-century Guildhall, old inns) walk south along the A458.
2. Take the first lane on the right (Callaughton). After ¾ mile turn right along a farm drive.
3. Keep on the track to swing right past a farm.
4. Climb up a rise to the B4378. In the valley below is Mary Webb's home, the Grange.
5. Turn left on the B4378. After ½ mile take the lane on the right. The path starts on the left after 300 yards. (If it is blocked keep on the B4378 to pick up the proper path through a gate on the right.)
6. The path becomes a hedged track to join the B4378. Turn right to Bourton.
7. At the crossroads turn right to climb Wenlock Edge and the B4371. In Corve Dale, a few miles to the left, is Wilderhope Manor.
8. Turn right on the B4371. Just past the junction a bridleway (rather hidden) starts on the left.
9. Keep along the clear track for 2 miles through the woods to a "green road".
10. The "road" goes by some old quarries to the B4371. Turn left to the A458 and Much Wenlock.

Mary — now growing visibly weaker and tormented by her husband's increasing infatuation with a girl student some 23 years his junior — replied kindly, and characteristically sent the Prime Minister a small bunch of violets "for your writing-table".

In the summer of 1927 Mary returned to Lyth Hill alone, and it was apparent to all who saw her that she was desperately ill. She sat in a chair by the wicket fence of her garden gazing out across the Shropshire landscape, occasionally adding to her final novel *Armour Wherein He Trusted*, but also composing some of her finest poetry. She returned to London in September, but was taken ill again and, desperately weak, went by train to a nursing home at St. Leonards-on-Sea, Sussex, where the family governess, Miss Lory, still lived in retirement. And there in a little room overlooking the English Channel she died a broken woman on 8th October, aged 46.

She was brought back in her coffin to Shropshire and buried underneath a lime tree in Shrewsbury cemetery, in full view of the hills she had loved. Friends and neighbours brought flowers from the fields, and from her cottage garden, to lay on her grave.

> *Under a blossoming tree*
> *Let me lie down,*
> *With one blackbird to sing to me*
> *In the evenings brown.*
> *Safe from the world's long importunity —*
> *The endless talk, the critical, sly stare,*
> *The trifling social days — and unaware*
> *Of all the bitter thoughts they have of me,*
> *Low in the grass, deep in the daisies,*
> *I shall sleep sound, safe from their blames and praises.*

Her death went virtually unreported at the time . . . few people in literary circles knew of it until the following spring when Prime Minister Baldwin, attending the Royal Literary Fund Society dinner at the Mansion House in London as guest speaker, surprised the entire gathering of eminent people, and the Press of the world, by embarking on an eulogy of Mary Webb, stating that in the opinion of John Buchan (*The Thirty-Nine Steps*, etc.) and Sir James Barrie (*Peter Pan*, etc.) she was "one of the three best writers of English today, but nobody buys her books".

Newspapers next day reported the Premier's praise in bold headlines, *The Times* even inserted a belated obituary — and Mary Webb's books sold in their hundreds of

Shrewsbury, to where Mary made a tragic return in 1927 . . .

Insight

Often a flash of sapphire in water, a shade of turquoise in the sky, will strike across the heart with an inexplicable pang. It is not sorrow; it is more than joy; it is at once the realisation of a perfect thing, the fear that we may never see it again, and the instinct that urges us to ascend through the known beauty to the unknown which is both the veil and the voice that summons beyond it.

M.W. from *Poems and the Spring of Joy*

thousands! Mary herself had died without leaving a will; her worldly assets totalled a mere £936. The following year, in September 1929, her husband — now wealthy as a result of the publishing of his wife's books — married the young lady he had been tutoring and they had two children. But ten years later, after making a lone and unexpected journey to the Lake District, he "fell" to his death from the top of 3,000ft Scafell. In his will he left £35,800 . . . and his young widow inherited the entire literary estate of Mary Webb. Later she married Jonathan Cape, the publisher.

Since then, Mary Webb's popularity has fluctuated in accordance with literary fashion. Hollywood made a film of *Gone To Earth* with Jennifer Jones in the leading rôle, but since the last war her name has gradually faded from the public eye.

But to those who enjoy seeking out the hidden beauties of the real English countryside, far from the crowded track of conventional tourism, the novels and poems of this curious woman of the hills are an open invitation . . . to discover and explore the brooding, romantic, and still unspoiled Shropshire world of Mary Webb.

The books of Mary Webb

The Golden Arrow (1916); Gone to Earth; The Spring of Joy (1917); The House in Dormer Forest (1920); Seven for a Secret (1922); Precious Bane (1924); Armour Wherein He Trusted (1929).

JOHN GALSWORTHY

(1867-1933)

Creator of one of literature's most famous families

John Galsworthy as a little baby in the arms of his mother, Blanche.

One's eyes are what one is,
One's mouth what one becomes.
J.G.

Four years before Victoria came to the Throne, old John Galsworthy — grandfather of the famous author — left his ancestral village near Plymouth Sound in Devon and went to London to seek his fortune. By hard work and a disciplined life he built up a lucrative practice as a lawyer in the capital. His eldest son, also called John, followed in his father's legal footsteps and by careful investment became a wealthy man of property and a pillar of the upper middle class which, by and large, ruled the England of its day.

It was into this world of privilege that the youngest John Galsworthy, destined to become one of the world's most celebrated novelists, was born during an August thunderstorm in the hot and humid summer of 1867. He grew up surrounded by the very people whose personalities and passions he would one day make famous as the Forsytes, a fictional name that could readily apply to the Galsworthys themselves. Their family story was, in truth, as intriguing and interesting as any episode in *The Forsyte Saga* which continues to command the rapt attention of readers the world over, nearly 60 years since the death of its creator.

The novelist's father — a highly respected London solicitor with kindly eyes and a full grey beard — was clearly the inspiration for Old Jolyon in the *Saga*. He built a red-bricked mansion at Coombe in Surrey (paralleled as Robin Hill in the novels) and his elder son, the young John, was born at nearby Parkfield on Kingston Hill while the family was preparing to move into the palatial home. John's early life was more concerned with nannies and governesses than with his parents, who entertained lavishly, and the young lad spent many evenings peeping through the banister rails

John Galsworthy, the great novelist and dramatist, who created and chronicled one of the most famous families in English literature — the Forsytes.

The school's coat of arms.

Harrow

Harrow! For the soldier, the
    traveller, the scout
Whether it be victory, or whether it
    be rout!
And when the fight is lost or won,
    and the dark camp is still
There shall be thought of the old
    songs and dreaming of the Hill.

JOHN GALSWORTHY

(published in the *Harrovian*, Dec. 21, 1929)

John Galsworthy senior. The novelist was devoted to his father and based the character of "Old Jolyon" in The Forsyte Saga on him.

The future novelist was a great success at sports whilst at Harrow, reaching the pinnacle of his school career by captaining the Football XI. He is the player in the front row with his foot on the ball.

from an upstairs landing as a glittering parade of dinner guests swept across the hall below . . . all the sights and sounds being carefully stored away in his childish memory to be later resurrected in the guise of the Forsytes.

John was sent away to prep school at Bournemouth when he was but nine years old and at 14 he went to Harrow where he learned the first commandment of an English gentleman — never be enthusiastic about anything, except cricket. This last was to remain a passion with him for life, especially the Eton-Harrow match at Lord's, an annual tradition which still continues. By 1884 John had become head of his house, captain of its football eleven, a member of the school cricket eleven, and winner of the School Mile — no mean feat. Even during his time at Harrow the characteristics which were to remain with him to his death were already apparent — his teachers noted him as a modest and unassuming boy, meticulously neat, who brought an unusual degree of seriousness to everything he tackled.

At Oxford, where he read law at New College, he was remembered as remarkably good-looking — tall, slender, fair haired and fastidiously dressed — if a little too solemn at times. He gained his degree in 1889 and was called to the bar the following spring. All seemed set for him to follow

John (standing second from right, wearing a bowler hat) with a group of fellow under-graduates of New College, Oxford, in 1888.

Writing

If one comes to ask oneself why anything is written one finds, doesn't one, that it is because certain emotions have been passed through, certain thoughts thought and certain feelings felt, and because there is in us that inspiring and at the same time pathetic desire that others should also know of and share these emotions, and thoughts and feelings. The logical result of this is that to be true and real one must express only what each of us has felt ... its value is its fidelity to ourselves, our convictions and our emotions, for only so does it go to the heart and convince others that a human being (a brother) like ourselves is speaking.

J.G.

the family tradition of entering and eventually heading a thriving law practice, but he failed to find any enthusiasm for his profession. Largely in an attempt to coax him into settling down his father sent him on a long overseas trip to Australia and the South Pacific in 1892, a time when Britain was enjoying the fruits of an Empire on which, it was rightly claimed, the sun never set.

It was while returning to England from this trip, aboard the famous clipper ship *Torrens*, that he met a man who was to have a lasting impact on his life. The ship's first mate — a swarthy looking foreigner speaking broken English — was Joseph Conrad. The arch-browed and spotlessly attired Galsworthy was somewhat repelled at first by Conrad's grimy appearance and rough ways, but after several long talks during the monotonous voyage back to the Cape the two became firm friends. Conrad had not at that stage published anything but the stories and anecdotes he told of his many adventures — later to be published in a galaxy of sea-faring novels — so appealed to Galsworthy that they fanned the flames of literary embers in the young Englishman's breast and on returning home, far from settling down to business as his father had hoped, he drifted listlessly while nurturing his secret ambition to write.

Then in stepped "Nemesis" — a woman with that as her

Joseph Conrad with his son Boris. It was his tales of adventure which stirred Galsworthy's imagination and literary ambitions.

45

A portrait of John in 1895 at the time of his first meeting with Ada (below). He wrote the following love poem for her.

To Ada

Lady, who in the yew shades lie,
Glancing up as I go by —
Lady! Long long will I love you!
Truer than the blue above you,
Softer than the South Wind
blowing,
Sweeter than the roses glowing,
Deeper than this dark yew tree,
So for you my love shall be.
Lady! You you are my Lady!

J.G.

unusual middle name. She was Ada Nemesis Galsworthy (née Cooper) married to John's first cousin, Arthur, a Guards officer. Ada, three years older than John, had revealed to his sisters, Lilian and Mabel, something of the brutish nature of her husband — this knowledge drew an immediate and ready sympathy from their compassionate and gentle brother. Hints of the cruelty Ada is believed to have suffered are contained in Galsworthy's final novel *Over the River*. The two met face to face on a Paris railway station in 1895 and it was Ada who crystallised John's thoughts in just a few words: "Why don't you write — you're just the person". Her opinion acted like a catalyst. John gave up law and, encouraged by the beautiful Ada, began to write in earnest.

Some of the feelings and frustrations both experienced can be gleaned from Galsworthy's early work. His first four books, all published under the nom-de-plume of "John Sinjohn", sold badly — but in one of his short stories Galsworthy introduced a character by the name of Soames Forsyte . . . a harbinger of triumphs to come. For his fifth and subsequent books Galsworthy dropped the pseudonym and used his own name and his growing attachment with Ada gave his writing a depth of feeling and experience he had previously lacked.

When John's father died in 1904 he and Ada left England together for an extended tour of the Continent, during which time divorce proceedings were instituted by Ada's husband. Old Mr. Galsworthy would not have countenanced such a stigma in the family, hence the couple waited till after his death . . . here was meat indeed for the personal crises that affected the Forsytes in Galsworthy's eventual work — the hard-headed Soames, his beautiful wife Irene, the interloping Bosinney . . . and the death of Old Jolyon. It was while on the Continent with Ada that John finished *The Man of Property*, first of the Forsyte novels, and they returned to England in September 1905 to be married on the very day that Ada's divorce decree became absolute.

In fact, the closeness of the fictional Forsytes to the real-life Galsworthys so alarmed several members of the family that John's sister Lilian wrote to him pleading for *The Man of Property* not to be published since she felt they were all so readily identifiable in it. But it appeared unaltered in March 1906 and was an immediate success.

The Forsyte family affairs — their successes, their failings,

A family portrait of the Galsworthys when John (on the right) was still a very young man. His father dominates the photograph in the centre, whilst sisters Lilian and Mabel are also in the back row.

their bickerings, possessiveness and perversity — caused a ripple of alarm in many an upper-middle-class-home and a flood of sniggers among those of the lower social orders. Dickens had written mainly of the Victorian poor and deprived with their wretched lives; Galsworthy concentrated on an entirely different genre. He wrote of the lives of the captains of industry in Edwardian England, the men of the government, and their wives. With consummate skill he took the lid off fashionable society for all to see.

His name shot up the literary ladder to equal, and in some cases surpass, the other lions of the times like H.G. Wells, Joseph Conrad, Arnold Bennett and Ford Madox Ford. He seemed all set for a dazzling future when, in addition to his books, his plays were playing to packed houses in London and the provinces. But as his success increased he found less and less time available for serious writing. Ada's love of the social round, her desire for frequent foreign travel and her apparently delicate health, all pulled him away from his main love — writing.

The couple lived at this time in Addison Road, Holland Park and Ada's social diary, in which she records some of the guests invited to dinner, reads like a *Who's Who* of Literature and Politics — George Bernard Shaw, John

Prayer

God of the daylights, love her,
And guard her tender ways!
Make gentle skies above her,
And give her sunny days!

God of the dark defend her,
And keep well in thy sight
Her happy feet, and send her
The kiss of sleep at night.

Scatter my ashes!
Hereby I make it a trust;
I in no grave be confined,
Mingle my dust with the dust,
Give me in fee to the wind!
Scatter my ashes.

If on a Spring night I went by
And God were standing there,
What is the prayer that I would cry
To Him? This is the prayer:
O God of Courage grave,
O Master of this night of spring!
Make firm in me a heart too brave
To ask Thee anything.

J.G.

Old Jolyon

The strange greetings over, old Jolyon seated himself on a wicker chair, and his two grandchildren, one on each side of his knees, looked at him silently, never having seen so old a man.

They were unlike, as though recognising the difference set between them by the circumstances of their births, Jolly, the child of sin, pudgy-faced, with his tow-coloured hair brushed off his forehead, and a dimple in his chin, had an air of stubborn amiability, and the eyes of a Forsyte; little Holly, the child of wedlock, was a dark-skinned, solemn soul, with her mother's grey and wistful eyes.

The dog Balthasar, having walked round the three small flower-beds, to show his extreme contempt for things at large, had also taken a seat in front of old Jolyon, and, oscillating a tail curled by Nature tightly over his back, was staring up with eyes that did not blink.

Even in the garden, that sense of things being pokey haunted old Jolyon; the wicker chair creaked under his weight; the garden-beds looked "daverdy"; on the far side, under the smut-stained wall, cats had made a path . . .

J.G. from *A Man of Property*

Masefield, W.H. Hudson, J.M. Barrie and E.V. Lucas; plus politicians of the stature of Asquith, Lloyd George, the Balfours and Winston Churchill. The list is not only an indication of the Galsworthys' social standing but also of Ada's success at courting friendship among the top names of the day and thereby putting behind her the stigma of having been born illegitimate and then going through an unseemly divorce action as the guilty party.

Ada's influence on Galsworthy cannot be overstated. She was constantly at his side in a super-secretarial rôle, scrutinising every page as he wrote it and expressing her opinion. Her close attention to his work was probably a severe restriction on his vision and style for he may well have tempered the power of his pen to meet Ada's approbation — or at least so as not to offend her highly sensitive social niceties. Galsworthy's success, however, was real enough as a novelist and playwright, in which fields he was perhaps the top literary earner of his day. But he was also a published poet, although his verse attracted scant attention and brought him even less financial reward.

While Ada thrived on London's social round, John found it near impossible to write there. He preferred to live and work in the country and, true to his roots, Devon most of all. In the spring of 1908 the couple took a lease on part of a farmhouse on the edge of Dartmoor — "Wingstone" in the village of Manaton. The house is described in his essay *Buttercup Night*, and it was there that he wrote some of his best work. While living there he occasionally visited the famous prison on Dartmoor and became a tireless campaigner for penal reform. Among other social causes he espoused were votes for women, slum clearance, anti-vivisection, cruelty to pit ponies, and children on the stage. It was at Wingstone that the Galsworthys spent most of the 1914-1918 war, John writing scores of essays, several novels, plays and many poems. He loathed violence in all its forms, writing of its horrors in many of his works.

As the war years rolled on with their ever-mounting carnage, Galsworthy despaired at what he saw as the ultimate demise of civilisation, or at least the end of orthodox Christianity. Although nearly 50 he volunteered for the Services but was rejected as unfit by a military tribunal. Yet he was still determined to do his "bit", although in an odd way, perhaps. To fulfil his desperate desire to help suffering humanity, particularly soldiers, he went to an army convalescent hospital in France in November 1916 to work as

Wingstone, Galsworthy's farmhouse near Manaton on the edge of Dartmoor.

Where my fathers stood
Watching the sea,
Gale-spent herring boats
Hugging the lea;
There my Mother lives,
Moorland and tree.
Sight o' the blossom!
Devon to me!

Where my fathers walked,
Driving the plough;
Whistled their hearts out—
Who whistles now?
There my Mother burns
Fire-faggots free.
Scent o' the wood-smoke!
Devon to me!

Where my fathers sleep,
Turning to dust,
This old body throw
When die I must!
There my Mother calls,
Wakeful is She!
Sounds o' the west-wind!
Devon to me!

Where my fathers lie,
When I am gone,
Who need pity me
Dead? Never one!
There my Mother clasps
Me. Let me be!
Feel o' the red earth!
Devon to me!

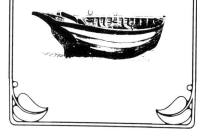

a masseur! Galsworthy, seeing at last a way in which he could help, took a crash course in Swedish massage, learning the manipulative process to ease the aching limbs and muscles of wounded men from the Front. As usual, and to her credit, Ada accompanied him to take care of the hospital linen, sewing and patching for many weary hours at a stretch.

The Galsworthys loved the work, hard though it was, and on their return to England in March 1917 John immediately set to work on *The Indian Summer of a Forsyte*, the forerunner of a chain of Forsyte episodes which were to culminate in the trilogy published in 1922 as *The Forsyte Saga*.

On New Year's Eve, 1917, while entertaining friends at Littlehampton, Galsworthy received a telegram from the Prime Minister, Lloyd George, stating: "Please wire by return whether you accept offer of knighthood".

"Sir John Galsworthy" . . . one can imagine how it rolled off Ada's refined tongue, at least mentally, when she read the telegram. But knowing her husband's view that no artist of letters ought to dally with titles and rewards of

The Seven Sisters in Sussex.

The Spell of England

by JOHN GALSWORTHY

I have sailed South to a new light,
New stars, and seen the Plough
Dip to the Cross, and watched the bright
Fish spraying from the prow.
Lagoons and palmgroves I have spied,
And loom of mangrove tree;
Yet craved for a salt heaven wide
Above the English sea.

I have been far afoot among
Old deserts and great hills,
And trailed across the forests long
That feed the lumber mills.
At memory of smiling Downs
Those grander visions pass,
For well I know to me the crown's
A day on English grass.

I have been mazed and mazed again
Where California glows,
And marvelled at a flowered Spain —
Her orange and her rose;
I've dreamed Japan, all cherry white;
Yet would I liefer see
The Springtime stars of blossom light
An English apple tree.

In many countries I have stood
Where miracles have thronged
To God's imaginative mood,
And yet my heart has longed
For English sound and scent and scene
Though all my reason knows
They'll never be, have never been
Fit to compare with those.

Why this should be, I cannot tell;
Of Man it seems decreed
That he shall feel the moving spell
Of his especial breed.
Muezzin call to night and morn —
"Brothers, near or far,
Be not dismayed that each is born
Under his native star!"

50

A notable gathering at Wingstone (from left to right): Granville Barker, Ada Galsworthy, George Bernard Shaw, Mrs. Shaw, John Galsworthy, Lilla McCarthy.

that nature, she might have been bitterly disappointed but not surprised when John wired back immediately: "Most profoundly grateful but feel I must not accept".

Nevertheless, next morning he found his name in the newspapers as a knight in the New Year's Honours List, forcing him to send a second wire to the Prime Minister confirming his refusal to accept. Given this stand against such honours it seems strange that, a few years later, in the Birthday Honours of June 1929, he felt able to accept the award of the Order of Merit, a similar honour having been accepted by Thomas Hardy whom Galsworthy knew.

In April 1918 Galsworthy became the editor of a government magazine then titled *Recalled to Life*. He immediately changed it to *Reveille*, a magazine that was entirely devoted to the needs and interests of disabled servicemen, and although he only headed the periodical for three issues he introduced the work of some famous contemporaries including Rudyard Kipling, W.E. Henley, Jerome K. Jerome and Robert Bridges and had the satisfaction of seeing the circulation jump to 30,000 copies despite its cover price of half-a-crown, a high one for those days.

In September 1918 the Galsworthys moved to Grove Lodge, Hampstead, from where Ada could continue her social round and John could ride his horse on the Heath

A man of action forced into a state of thought is unhappy until he can get out of it.   J.G.

Youth's Own

Out of the fields I see them pass,
Youth's own battalion —
Like moonlight ghosting over grass,
To dark oblivion.

They have a solemn tryst to keep
Out on the starry heath;
To fling them down, and sleep
  and sleep
Beyond Reveille — Death!

    J.G.

John and Ada Galsworthy on their camels during a visit to Egypt in 1914.

Prayer

God, I am travelling out to death's
    sea,
I, who exulted in sunshine and
    laughter,
Thought not of dying — death is
    such a waste of me!
Grant me one prayer: Doom not
    the hereafter
Of mankind to war, as though I had
    died not—
I, who in battle, my comrade's arm
    linking,
Shouted and sang — life in my
    pulses hot
Throbbing and dancing! Let not
    my sinking
In dark be for naught, my death a
    vain thing!
God, let me know the end of
    man's fever!
Make my last breath a bugle call,
    carrying
Peace o'er the valleys and cold hills
    for ever!

J.G.

every morning, although they kept the lease on the Devon farmhouse until 1923. Three years later John could bear being cut off from the country no longer and bought Bury House, a 15-bedroomed Tudor-style mansion near Pulborough in Sussex. In 1917, when Galsworthy himself was 60, he wrote *Swan Song* and much to the regret of his world-wide public decided to kill-off his most illustrious character Soames Forsyte. This spelt the end of the *Saga*, although he produced a later book in 1930 of apocryphal Forsyte tales, and there followed a lightweighted trilogy of books on the fictional Cherrell family, but nothing to match the calibre of the Forsytes.

His health, which had been strong throughout his life, began to fail as he approached his 65th birthday and when in November of 1932 he heard that he had been awarded the highest honour for any writer — the Nobel Prize for Literature — he had every intention of travelling to Stockholm to receive the Prize and deliver a lecture in the December. But this was not to be and he died at his Hampstead home on 31st January, 1933. Ada, who had always been of great concern to him because of her constantly poor health, lived on for a further 20 years. They had no children.

In marked contrast to world opinion at the time Galsworthy considered himself to be a failure — not, of course, in the financial sense for his books ran into millions

The novelist and his wife in 1930.

and his plays were constantly being produced and applauded — but in the quality and style of his writing. Life, he felt, had been over-generous to him and had he faced severe hardship and deprivation, perhaps, his work would have taken a different direction and had greater social impact. He alone felt that his best creative effort was to be found in his verse, the most fulfilling literary medium for him. He was his own severest critic and did not enjoy the adulation that increasingly came his way. He would have much preferred to be another W.H. Hudson, the man of letters he admired the most.

Galsworthy had the rare talent of being able to shut himself off from the world around him, whether in hotel room or train, take out his blotter pad and straight pen and write. He saw and recorded the doings of the Forsytes because he was one himself. But most of all he wrote of England and the English people he mixed with. Because he himself was a very fine Englishman.

The Novels of John Galsworthy

From the Four Winds (1897); Jocelyn (1898); Villa Rubein (1900); A Man of Devon (1901); The Island Pharisees (1904); The Man of Property (1906); The Country House (1907); Fraternity (1909); The Patrician (1911); The Dark Flower (1913); The Freelands (1915); Beyond (1917); The Burning Spear (1919); In Chancery (1920); To Let (1921); The Forsyte Saga (a trilogy comprising The Man of Property, In Chancery and To Let) (1922); The White Monkey (1924); The Silver Spoon (1926); Two Forsyte Interludes (1927); Swan Song (1928); On Forsyte Change (1930); Maid in Waiting (1931); Flowering Wilderness (1932); Over the Rover (1933).

W.H. DAVIES

(1871-1940)

The tramp-poet who found "time to stand and stare"

The Likeness

When I came forth this morn I saw
Quite twenty cloudlets in the air;
And then I saw a flock of sheep,
Which told me how those clouds came there.

That flock of sheep, on the green grass,
Well might it lie so still and proud,
Its likeness had been drawn in heaven,
On a blue sky, in silvery cloud.

I gazed me up, I gazed me down,
And swore, though good the likeness was,
'Twas a long way from justice done
To such white wool, such sparkling grass.

W.H.D.

Tramps and beggars were a common sight in England earlier this century, the numbers of itinerants having been swollen by wounded ex-servicemen invalided out of the forces. Therefore little attention would have been given to a small, broad-shouldered pedlar with a wooden leg stumping his way through the Midlands in 1904 with a tray of boot-laces, pins and needles. But the stories of his travels, both here and in America and Canada, were soon to capture the attention of the world. For the one-legged pedlar was W.H. Davies, the "super-tramp" whose autobiography soared to success as a literary legend and whose simple, unconventional and seemingly effortless poetry became a classic of its kind.

William Henry Davies was born in July 1871 at the Church House tavern in Newport, Monmouthshire — a border county once administered as part of England. His father having died while he was still a baby, and his mother soon remarrying, young William was brought up, together with his sister and mentally retarded brother, by their paternal grandparents, a retired Cornish sea captain and his wife.

Bright at school — he passed all his exams with ease — young William served an apprenticeship as a picture-framer in Bristol, but still found time to study the works of the great poets, Shakespeare, Byron, Shelley and Keats. Even as a young man he began writing verse of his own, but chronic shyness — which afflicted him throughout his life — prevented his showing it to anyone else.

On completion of his strictly indentured apprenticeship he decided to throw up a steady career as a tradesman in

W.H. Davies in the garden of his home at Nailsworth in Gloucestershire.

Cuckoo Day

The woods and banks of England
now,
Late coppered with dead leaves and
old,
Have made the early violets grow,
And bulge with knots of primrose
gold.
Hear how the blackbird flutes away,
Whose music scorns to sleep at night:
Hear how the cuckoo shouts all day
For echoes — to the world's delight:
Hullo, you imp of wonder, you —
Where are you now, cuckoo? Cuckoo?

W.H.D.

A portrait of the poet whose shy manner disguised a life which was full of adventure and incident.

order to see the world. With his meagre savings, and £15 from the legacy of his grandmother who had just died, he set sail for America in 1895. Inevitably, and predictably, he quickly exhausted his funds and was obliged by circumstances to become a tramp in order to find work. Over the next five years he rode the U.S. railroads as a hobo, occasionally being employed as a fruit picker and casual labourer, but more often than not living from hand to mouth as one of the vast army of unemployed migrants that roamed America at the turn of the century.

The richness of his experiences, allied to his natural gift for story-telling, eventually found expression in his unique volume *The Autobiography of a Super Tramp*. Published in 1908, it was his first prose work and rocketed him to fame. The book became part of the syllabus in schools throughout the world and a certain bestseller among boys of all ages.

Davies wrote candidly of his many exploits, and of the

characters he met — Cockney More, Irish Tim and Australian Red. Once, while on his way across Canada to join in the Klondyke gold rush with a fellow tramp called "Three-Fingered Jack", Davies leapt for the running-board of a train moving out of Renfrew, Ontario. He slipped and his right ankle was crushed, resulting in an eventual amputation below the knee.

This forced his return to England, on crutches, and with the money accruing to him from his grandmother's legacy of ten shillings a week he bought himself an artificial limb and went to London, staying in common lodging houses (cost, fourpence a night) while writing poetry and trying to get his work published. When this failed — no-one, it seemed, wanted to buy poetry from a tramp at the door — he walked on his wooden leg through the Midlands, into South Wales and then down to Devon and Cornwall before returning to London, peddling laces and sewing requisites to scratch a living. In so doing he learned the art of begging and, as he was later to describe in his *Autobiography*, discovered the peculiar language and habits of the vagrant community.

His *feather* (bed for the night) cost 16 farthings (fourpence) and he would need a little more to pay for *scrand* (food) and *skimish* (drink). He was ridiculed for selling *stretchers* (laces) and *sharps* (needles), but at least that was considered better than grinding *sniffs* (scissors), for this latter class of itinerant was regarded with scorn and hostility.

The élite of the begging profession was shared by the *gridler* — a man who wandered from street to street singing hymns and old ballads, to a cascade of pennies thrown from upper windows — and the *downrighter*, one who refused to sell anything, preferring instead to approach passers-by with a straight request for assistance. This last required nerve plus some degree of eloquence. Such a one as Davies, given to shyness, could not consider it, but he admits to helping a gridler pick up pennies in the street.

Little of the anguish and heartache of such a life was revealed by Davies, but doubtlessly one major setback was his failure to be able to borrow books from the public library. During his time as a tramp he could not call upon even one ratepayer to sign his library application form as a reference. Nevertheless, by means of begging and peddling, plus his weekly legacy, he saved enough money to have his first book of poems published in 1905, and sent them unsolicited through the post to well-known people,

Sweet Stay-at-Home

Sweet Stay-at-Home, sweet
    Well-content,
Thou knowest of no strange
    continent:
Thou hast not felt thy bosom keep
A gentle motion with the deep;
Thou hast not sailed in Indian seas,
Where scent comes forth in every
    breeze.
Thou hast not seen the rich grape
    grow
For miles, as far as eyes can go;
Thou hast not seen a summer's night
When maids could sew by a worm's
    light;
Nor the North Sea in spring send
    out
Bright hues that like birds flit about
In solid cages of white ice—

Sweet Stay-at-Home, sweet
    Love-one-place.
Thou hast not seen black fingers
    pick
White cotton when the bloom is
    thick,
Nor heard black throats in harmony;
Nor hast thou sat on stones that lie
Flat on the earth, that once did rise
To hide proud kings from common
    eyes,
Thou hast not seen plains full of
    bloom
Where green things had such little
    room
They pleased the eye like fairy
    flowers—
Sweet Stay-at-Home, all these long
    hours.
Sweet Well-content, sweet
    Love-one-place,
Sweet simple maid, bless thy dear
    face;
For thou hast made more homely
    stuff
Nurture thy gentle self enough;
I love thee for a heart that's kind—
Not for the knowledge in thy mind.

                    W.H.D.

The country poet Edward Thomas who was immediately impressed with Davies's verse and became a close friend and staunch supporter of the "super-tramp".

inviting them to purchase a copy at half–a–crown or return the book. In this way he disposed of some 60 or so copies out of a print of more than 200.

Among the recipients was a then controversial Irish playwright, George Bernard Shaw, who immediately recognised the merit of Davies's work and became actively concerned in promoting the tramp poet's interests. At Shaw's suggestion Davies sent copies of his book to the poet Edward Thomas, St. John Adcock, editor of the *Bookman* magazine, and others. Favourable reviews began to appear in literary journals, including one by Arnold Bennett, and when a London newspaper wrote up the story of Davies's life, success and fame swiftly followed.

Edward Thomas was a particular friend, although in straitened cicumstances himself. He found a small cottage for Davies at Sevenoaks in Kent and, with friends, paid for the rent, coal and light. It was at Sevenoaks that Davies was able to write his famous *Autobiography*, which was published with a glowing preface by Shaw who spoke of his impressions after reading Davies's poems for the first time:

> "Before I had read three lines I perceived that the author was a real poet. His work was not in the least strenuous or modern . . . there was no sign of his ever having read anything otherwise than as a child reads. The result was a freedom from literary vulgarity which was like a draught of clear water in a desert. Here, I saw, was a genuine innocent, writing odds and ends of verse about odds and ends of things, living quite out of the world in which such things are usually done."

Of the *Autobiography* Shaw went on to say:

> "I have read it through from beginning to end, and would have read more had there been any more to read. It is a placid narrative, unexciting in matter and unvarnished in manner, of the commonplaces of a tramp's life. It is of a very curious quality."

From then until the outbreak of the Second World War in 1939, Davies published a score of little poetry books, and when his collected verse was eventually issued in 1943 it contained the astonishing total of 636 different poems! In addition, he wrote four novels continuing the autobiographic nature of his tramping life. In 1923 he wrote *True Travellers*, which he sub-titled "A Tramp's Opera in Three Acts". This was to have been produced at the Lyric theatre, Hammersmith, where John Gay's *The Beggar's Opera* achieved its success two centuries earlier, but the

The Gridler

by W.H. Davies

"Now," said this man, "to business; for we must get the price of our beds and a little breakfast for the morning, not to mention the night's supper. All you have to do," he said again, "is to pick up the coppers as they come."

Wondering what these words could mean, I followed him, on this pleasant afternoon, up several side streets, until we came to the end of one very long street, which had respectable looking houses on either side of the road. My strange companion walked several yards down this street, and then came to a sudden halt in the middle of the road.

"Now," said he, for the third or fourth time, "all you have to do is to pick up the coppers. I ask you to do no more; except," he added, grinning rather unpleasantly, "except to see that we are not picked up by the coppers."

His joke appeared simple enough, and I could not fail to understand it, but it was not all to my relish. The last named coppers were police officers, who would be likely to take hold of us for illegally appropriating the copper coins of the realm.

"Are you going to pick up the coppers?" he asked me a little impatiently, seeing me standing irresolute and undecided as to what to do. Scarcely knowing how to answer him, I said that if I saw any coppers he need have no fear but that I would pick them up.

"All right, that's good," he said, at the same time moving several feet away from me. I stood still watching these mysterious movements, and thinking of the coppers, wondering from what source they would be supplied. He now turned his back, without more ado, and, setting his eyes

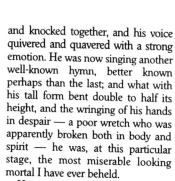

on the front windows before him, began, to my amazement, to sing a well-known hymn, singing it in the most horrible and life-less voice I have ever heard.

In spite of the drink, which had now taken effect, making my head swell with stupidity, I still felt an overwhelming shame at finding myself in this position. I stood irresolute, not knowing whether to wait the result of this, or to leave him at once with short ceremony. But whilst ruminating in this frame of mind, I heard a window open with a loud creak, saw the shaking of a fair hand, and then heard a copper coin fall on the hard earth within a yard of where I stood. Being penniless I was nothing loth to take possession of this coin, and had scarcely done so, when a front door opened on the other side of the street, and a fat florid old gentleman appeared and beckoned me across to him. Going immediately to this gentleman, I received twopence and, after thanking him, joined my companion in the road.

Now, as I belong to a race of people that are ever prone to song, whether it be in a public house or a prayer meeting, it will not suprise many to know that ere long I was making strong attempts to sing bass to this man's miserable treble, and only ceased to do so when it became necessary to stoop and pick up the coppers, which continued to come in at a rate of two to the minute. The effect of my voice on my companion was immediately apparent. His limbs shook, his knees bent

and knocked together, and his voice quivered and quavered with a strong emotion. He was now singing another well-known hymn, better known perhaps than the last; and what with his tall form bent double to half its height, and the wringing of his hands in despair — a poor wretch who was apparently broken both in body and spirit — he was, at this particular stage, the most miserable looking mortal I have ever beheld.

He was in this old man's broken attitude when, to my surprise, he suddenly straightened his great body, and gazed about one second down the street. After which he quickly turned on his heels, saying, in short peremptory tones — "Quick march", at the same time suiting the action to the words, in sharp military steps. What the people in their different windows, and on their doors, thought of this change, I cannot say. I looked down the street, and then saw that a police officer had just turned its far corner, and was coming slowly in our direction.

—— from 'The Autobiography of a Super Tramp' ——

Emma, the poet's wife. The unusual background to their life together was an incredible story in itself.

Rich Days

Welcome to you, rich Autumn days,
Ere comes the cold, leaf-picking wind;
When golden stocks are seen in fields,
All standing arm-in-arm entwined;
And gallons of sweet cider seen
On trees in apples red and green.

With mellow pears that cheat our
    teeth,
Which melt that tongues may suck
    them in;
With blue-black damsons, yellow
    plums,
Now sweet and soft from stone to
    skin;
And woodnuts rich, to make us go
Into the loneliest lanes we know.

W.H.D.

scheme fell through. In 1919 he was granted a Civil List pension and a few years later the University of Wales conferred upon him the honorary degree of Doctor of Literature . . . and so the super-tramp might have been expected to mature and plod blissfully through the rest of his life as convention dictates. But no . . . he took a further secret with him to the grave.

This concerned his marriage in 1923 to Helen Matilda Payne, daughter of a Sussex farmer. Davies was then over 50 and Helen, whom he always called Emma, was barely out of her teens. That the union was happy there is no doubt, despite the great difference in their ages, for Davies recorded and reflected his marital joy in *The Lover's Song Book*, published in 1933. But what the reference books do not reveal was that Davies, thwarted at finding a wife from conventional sources and society, elected to choose one from the streets of London. It was to be more in the nature of a rescue, a planned attempt to salvage at least one of the capital's unfortunate women, give her the respectability of marriage, and the chance of a new life in the green of England's countryside.

The facts — only recently revealed — bear some resemblance to the theme of Shaw's famous play *Pygmalion*, which eventually was used as the basis of the musical *My Fair Lady*, and given the earlier connection between the two writers one can only guess at where Davies first obtained his idea.

The secret of Emma's background was unknown to any of their friends, but Davies himself wrote it down in manuscript, sending it to his publishers (Jonathan Cape) in 1924 with the proviso that if it were to be published it should be done so anonymously and not attributed to him.

The publishers sent the manuscript to Shaw to read and although calling it an "amazing document" he advised against publishing it as it might harm Davies's literary reputation. By this time Davies himself had had second thoughts and wrote to Capes asking them to return the original manuscript, which they did, and destroy the two typewritten copies. However, this last was not done and the copies remained in the firm's safe for over 50 years, largely forgotten, until both Davies and his wife were dead. It was published in 1980 under the title *Young Emma*.

After their marriage the couple lived in Oxted, Surrey, and in 1931 moved to the small Gloucestershire town of

Cows with time to stare . . . early evening near Crummock Water in the lovely Lake District.

Leisure

by W.H. Davies

What is this life if, full of care,
We have no time to stand and stare.
No time to stand beneath the boughs
And stare as long as sheep or cows.
No time to see, when woods we pass,
Where squirrels hide their nuts in grass.
No time to see, in broad daylight,
Streams full of stars, like skies at night.
No time to turn at Beauty's glance,
And watch her feet, how they can dance.
No time to wait till her mouth can
Enrich that smile her eyes began.
A poor life this if, full of care,
We have no time to stand and stare.

W.H. Davies Remembered

I was only a lad at the time when W.H. Davies rented a cottage from my father at the village of Weald, near Sevenoaks, Kent. My first remembrance of things was about the long meadow nearby. The stile at the bottom seemed a favourite seat for Davies. As the cows were here, we have often thought it could have been this scene which inspired him to write his poem Leisure:

What is this life if, full of care,
We have no time to stand and stare?
No time to stand beneath the boughs
And stare as long as sheep or
cows . . .

Once, when my father was out visiting, Davies came out of the door of his cottage just as my father was passing. He held a poker in one hand and a watch dangling on its chain in the other. He said to my father, "I can't get this thing to go, so I was just going to throw it into the pond, then I thought I would always think about it on passing, so would your boy like it for a plaything?"

Well, my father thought the watch too good for that so he took it to Sydney Smith, a watch man in Tonbridge, who got it going. Father gave the watch, a "Climax", to me to keep. I still have this watch, although it no longer works now, but I wore it for years and it was always a good time-keeper.

My father went to Hildenborough Station with horse and farm waggon at times, to take apples for Covent Garden market. Once Davies asked if he would collect a parcel for him which was due. Father collected it and brought it back, thinking at the time what a strange shape it was. A day or two afterwards, Davies showed him what had been in the parcel — a new artificial leg for him!

F.C. BARROW

(From a letter published in the Autumn 1984 issue of *This England*)

The little stone cottage in the Golden Valley of Gloucestershire where the tramp-poet lived out his final days.

Nailsworth which nestles in the Golden Valley of the south Cotswolds, and only a few miles as the crow flies from the poet's native Newport across the Severn.

The roving spirit which had characterised Davies's early life was still in evidence after the move west for in the last eight years of his life he lived in four different houses in Nailsworth, yet all within a short distance of each other. Although he was not a great social mixer, not wishing to be fêted as a literary celebrity in so small a town, he was not an uncommon figure in the streets and some older locals still recall him — short of stature, broad-chested and with a skin darkened by his love of the outdoor life — the stiffness of his walk being the only tell-tale sign of his disability.

He was more often to be found in his garden, smoking his pipe, enjoying the sights, sounds and smells of Nature, and waiting for poetic inspiration "like a black cat waiting patiently at a mousehole", he used to say. However, he allowed his garden to become weed-choked, preferring Nature's arrangements to man's, but this did not hinder him writing two of his most popular prose works, *My Birds* and, later, *My Garden*.

After suffering a stroke in the late Thirties, from which he almost wholly recovered, he died childless at Nailsworth in September 1940. Emma survived him by almost 40 years, dying in 1979, apparently unaware that the secret of her early life was soon to be revealed.

A view of Nailsworth, final home of W.H. Davies after a life of wandering.

A portrait of W.H. Davies by Dame Laura Knight.

Doubtless their years in Gloucestershire had been idyllic, for it was at Nailsworth that Davies put his simple philosophy into these few lines:

> *With this small house, this garden large,*
> *This little gold, this lovely mate,*
> *With health in our body, peace at heart —*
> *Show me a man more great.*

Jacob Epstein sculpted a bust in bronze of Davies, which now rests in the Newport Art Gallery, and there are numerous portraits of him, one painted by Augustus John hanging in the University of Wales, and others by Dame Laura Knight and Sir William Rothenstein. But the best remembrance by far is his work, particularly the delicacy and perfection of his happy, lilting verse. He composed his poetry effortlessly as he ambled along life's highway because he wrote down the simple thoughts that sprang from his own daily doings. Despite his humble beginnings, and tragic misfortune along the way, Davies never let the world and its tragedies or triumphs deflect him from the path he chose to take . . . indeed he was one man who, in this life full of care, did find time to stand and stare.

The Works of W.H. Davies

The Soul's Destroyer (1905); Farewell to Poesy; The Autobiography of a Super Tramp (1908); Nature Poems; Beggars (1909); New Poems; Nature; Song of Joy; The Song of Life; The True Traveller (1912); Child Lovers; Foliage and Other Poems; The Hour of Magic; Shorter Lyrics of the 20th Century (1922); True Travellers: A Tramp's Opera (1923); Secrets; Later Days (1925); A Poet's Alphabet; The Adventures of Johnny Walker, Tramp (1926); The Bird of Paradise; The Song of Love; Dancing Mad; A Poet's Calendar; A Poet's Pilgrimage; Ambition and Other Poems; Jewels of Song; A Pilgrimage in Wales; Poems 1930-31; My Birds; My Garden; The Lover's Song Book (1933); Love Poems (1935); The Birth of Song; An Anthology of Short Poems; The Loneliest Mountain; The Essential W.H. Davies; The Complete Poems (1943); Young Emma (1980).

FLORA THOMPSON

(1876-1947)

The country girl whose life story became a classic

Lark Rise

The hamlet stood on a gentle rise in the flat wheat-growing north-east corner of Oxfordshire. We will call it Lark Rise because of the great number of skylarks which made the surrounding fields their springboard and nested on the bare earth between the rows of green corn . . . *from Lark Rise by Flora Thompson*

T owards the end of the last century a gypsy woman entered the tiny post office in a small Oxfordshire village. She needed to send a letter to a distant relative, but she had never learned to write. So the willowy young girl behind the counter cheerfully obliged her, as she had often done before to the many illiterates with whom she came into contact. By way of thanks, the gypsy offered to tell the young girl's fortune:

The fortune was pleasing. Whoever heard of one that was not? There was no fair man or dark man or enemy to beware of in it, and though she promised Laura love, it was not love of the usual kind.

"You're going to be loved," she said; "loved by people you've never seen and never will see."

A graceful way of thanking one for writing a letter . . .

The old gypsy's words were to prove uncannily accurate. For Laura, the girl behind the post office counter, was Flora Thompson, a gentle and tender child of humble birth whose wistful and modest appearance hid a rare literary genius. Not until she was 62 was her first book published, and she died at the age of 70, alone and largely unaware of the acclaim her work was eventually to receive, and the love for her it was to generate among her admirers the world over. Even now, more than a century after her birth, she is still comparatively little known, but many of those who have "discovered" her minor classic, the semi-autobiography *Lark Rise to Candleford*, have gone on pilgrimage to her native North Oxfordshire hamlet, and the villages and undulating countryside around, to soak in at first hand the atmosphere and aura of a part of England that is now rightly being called "Flora Thompson Country".

Flora Thompson, the gentle and quiet country writer who during her lifetime could never have imagined how popular her books would one day become.

County Cameos

Dorset is a dairy-maid, all curds and cream and roses. Wiltshire, a princess of the Stone Age, fugitive, aloof. You may tread her vast open spaces and breathe her pollen-scented air for a month, and never once catch a glimpse of her; although the most ancient of counties, she still awaits her poet to interpret her, or perhaps she crowned him such ages ago that his very language has faded from man's memory.

Then Sussex, with her springy thyme-turf, the pearly white of her Downs and the dim, distant blue of her wealdlands. But ask the Sussex people about her! Every man of them who can hold a pen has written at least one book about his own particular town or village; they teach their babes in school to sing her praises, and draw the very place-names out into a song! But Hampshire, dear, warm, tender Hampshire! Very few have praised her. Yet she is most worthy; a dark Madonna, with heather-purple robe and deep pine-tresses, sitting in the sun with a blessing for all who seek her.

F.T. from "August" in *A Country Calendar*

The "End House" at Juniper Hill where Flora lived as a child.

This was an England of stuffed chine, harvest-home suppers and songs, Sunday schools, zinc baths, squires in mellow tweeds and their ladies in fruity hats; a time when country wives brought up ten children on as many shillings a week, when a pig was an important member of the family and when "nervous troubles" had yet to be invented.

In the last ten years of her life, Flora Thompson sat down to write everything that she remembered of her childhood, and from her needle-sharp memory poured a torrent of detail about the daily lives of the "bettermost-poor" in the last two decades of the 19th century. She only knew poverty, in one form or another, all her life, but she turned it to good account nearly fifty years later in writing her best-selling works. She forgot nothing . . . the children's games, the old wives' tales, the men's drinking songs, all are there to savour and relish, told at first hand by an authoress of outstanding talents.

In a radio broadcast tribute in 1956, the well-known biographer Margaret Lane said:

> "Flora Thompson is one of those rare small geniuses who create one perfect thing in a lifetime and never attempt, or perhaps are not really capable of, another . . . It really seems as though her whole life, and her whole talent, had prepared her for a single task; that she found out just in time what that task was, and performed it. I don't really believe that if she had lived longer, or begun earlier, she would have produced a larger body of work of this excellence."

The church at Cottisford which Flora attended as a girl.

It was in the tiny hamlet of Juniper Hill in north-east Oxfordshire, only a few hundred yards from the border with Northamptonshire that Flora Jane Timms was born on 5th December, 1876. She was the eldest of six children of an Oxford stonemason, Albert Timms, who settled in the hamlet after marrying Emma Lapper, a nursemaid from a nearby rectory.

There were some two dozen cottages in Juniper Hill, which Flora renamed "Lark Rise" in her book, built more or less in a circle, and just over a mile from the mother village of Cottisford (renamed Fordlow by Flora) where the church and school were situated. Flora's childhood home was known as "the End House", built facing the cornfields with its back door towards the other cottages. This fact alone set the Timms family apart from the rest of the hamlet — but there were other reasons. Flora's father was, except for the innkeeper, the only man not employed as an agricultural labourer, the wage for which was 10 shillings a week. He earned a trifle more — probably 12 shillings — but had to walk three miles each way every day to Brackley (Northants) to his job with a local building firm.

Albert Timms was not liked in the hamlet, mainly because he was a brooding malcontent, considering himself a cut above the others, and claiming to have come from a "good" family before circumstances brought them down in the world. Yet like his father before him his drinking habits were to keep his own family poorer than they otherwise would have been. He once described Juniper Hill as "the spot God made with the left-overs when He'd finished

To be born in poverty is a terrible handicap to a writer. I often say to myself that it has taken one lifetime for me to prepare to make a start. If human life lasted two hundred years I might hope to accomplish something.

F.T.

On the Hill

When I reached the summit of the hill this morning there was no sight or sound of any life excepting my own. The air there was clearer and sharper; the crest of the hill seemed to rise like a pine-crowned island from a white and woolly sea. A pigeon cleaving the waves a dozen yards down appeared from above rather to swim than fly. At intervals from the misty sea rose the dark plumes of pine-tops, like other islands, but they were far below and infinitely remote.

Up there, cut off by the white enveloping mist, one seemed to be entirely out of the world. The wind, never absolutely silent where there are pine trees, had sunk to a sigh; the long-drawn wailing of new-born lambs from the valley fold came faintly as from another sphere. To listen intently was to hear the dull roar of silence.

F.T. from "January" in *A Country Calendar*

Cottisford School in about 1904 with the School Inspector's car standing outside.

creating the rest of the earth", but he never left the hamlet, dying there an embittered man long after Flora had left home.

Flora was a "loner" like her father. She learned to read before going to school and was often to be seen walking about the hamlet on her own with a book in her hand, a practice frowned upon by the other mothers. She was a gentle, slender child with pale yellow hair and unusually dark eyes, an odd combination it was said. She had a deep love for Nature and, for a peasant child, a keen observation for all things around her. She hated crowds and noise, and dreaded the daily walk to school with the rough-and-tumble children of the hamlet. At school she was, she claimed, "permanently at the bottom of the class" — poor at needlework and arithmetic, but good at reading and writing. In later life she was able to extend her village school education by joining the Free Library and reading Greek and Roman classics.

Flora's mother, a fair, small and pretty woman, had learned better manners and standards than the average village wife through her years of service at Fewcott Rectory, and she was a mine of old country sayings and songs, many of which are brought to life in Flora's writings. Her mother was a strict disciplinarian, and Flora referred later to a

68

Inside Cottisford School where Flora said she was "permanently at the bottom of the class".

somewhat harsh and restricted childhood for herself and Edwin, her beloved younger brother, called Edmund in her book. In *Lark Rise* she writes:

> Perhaps being of mixed birth with a large proportion of peasant blood in them, they were tougher in fibre than some. When their bottoms were soundly smacked, as they often were, their reaction was to make a mental note not to repeat the offence which had caused the smacking, rather than lay up for themselves complexes to spoil their later lives.

Humble though it was, Flora loved her two-up and two-down thatched cottage home, with its green painted door and a plum tree trained up the stone walls. And when she left it at the age of 14, to begin her adult life as an assistant in the post office at Fringford village (called Candleford Green in her books), there were tears in her eyes as she was being driven away by her father in a borrowed spring-cart.

She spent five happy years at the village post office-cum-blacksmith's forge at Fringford, learning rapidly the whole complicated postal business even to delivering letters, which often involved long walks through field, forest and country lanes. Before reaching the age of twenty Flora left Fringford to work as relief postmistress in various villages before moving in 1897 to the post office at Grayshott in Surrey. It was here that she met many of the literary giants

I fear that much of the salt of the earth will be lost in the process of transforming the old, sturdy, independent type of farm labourer into the proletariat. The only hope is that the countryman's roots are so strong and so well down in the soil that, after this terrible time is over, the country virtues will spring anew.

F.T.

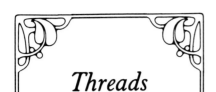

Threads

As she went on her way, gossamer threads, spun from bush to bush, barricaded her pathway, and as she broke through one after another of these fairy barricades she thought, "They're trying to bind and keep me." But the threads which were to bind her to her native county were more enduring than gossamer. They were spun of love and kinship and cherished memories.

F.T. from *Candleford Green*

Flora with her daughter in 1905.

The post office at Fringford, Oxfordshire, renamed "Candleford Green" in her writings, where Flora began her working life and (opposite page) the blacksmith's forge which was next door.

of the day who lived in the area, for they were frequent users of the mails — including Sir Arthur Conan Doyle, Grant Allen and George Bernard Shaw. She later wrote of this episode:

I used to listen to their conversations, meeting and greeting each other at my counter, myself as unregarded as a piece of furniture, but noting all.

Perhaps these "great examples" encouraged my desire to express myself in writing, but I cannot remember the time when I did not wish and mean to write. My brother (Edwin) and I used to make up verses and write stories and diaries from our earliest years, and I had never left off writing essays for the pleasure of writing. No one saw them; there was no one likely to be interested."

She was wrong, but it was not until many years after she had met and married her husband — John William Thompson, a postal clerk from Aldershot — and the birth of her first two children, Winifred and Basil, that she began writing in earnest. The *Titanic* disaster in 1912 had prompted a Scottish poet, Ronald Campbell Macfie, to write an ode which was published in *The Literary Monthly*, and readers were invited to send in critical essays about it as the basis of a competition. Flora's essay won the first prize and this led to a long friendship with Dr. Macfie, a physician, who encouraged Flora's literary bent for almost 20 years until his death in 1931.

The blacksmith's forge at Fringford.

Heather

You talk of pale primroses,
Of frail and fragrant posies,
The cowslip and the cuckoo-flower
    that scent the spring-time lea.
But give to me the heather,
The honey-scented heather,
The glowing gypsy heather —
That is the flower for me!

You love the garden alleys,
Smooth-shaven lawns and valleys,
The cornfields and the shady lane,
    and fisher-sails at sea.
But give to me the moorland,
The noble purple moorland,
The free, far-stretching moorland —
That is the land for me!

              F.T.

Her first published essay —another competition winner, published in 1916 — was on the works of Jane Austen, whom she admired greatly, and this led to other articles being accepted by newspapers and magazines. She wrote a regular Nature series for 20 years in the *Catholic Fireside*, a weekly magazine, although she had no connection with that faith in the past, and this gave rise to correspondence which was to have a profound effect upon her later life. The *Daily News*, once edited by Charles Dickens, began publishing her works, as did *Chamber's Journal*, the *Lady* and various smaller newspapers at home and abroad.

The death of her beloved brother Edwin, killed in action in Belgium in 1916, grieved Flora so deeply that she momentarily lost the will to write. That year the Thompsons moved from Bournemouth, where they had lived since their marriage, to the post office at Liphook, Hampshire, and in 1918 her third child, Peter, was born when she was aged 41 and had thought her days of motherhood were over.

In 1921 Flora had her book of verse published under the title *Bog Myrtle and Peat*, a collection of her poetry which, alas, failed to sell well and can be adjudged a commercial failure. Three years later she founded the Peverel Society, a postal association for literary aspirants, and this occupied her time for some 18 years in which she coached and criticised the members in prose and verse.

Flora's brother Edwin who was killed in the First World War.

Caroline and Mrs. Pulbrook

Charity remembered them well and saw them again in imagination: Mrs. Pulbrook, large, pink-cheeked and placid-looking, when untroubled by her foe, and Caroline, about five feet high and dark as a gypsy, with snaky curls and spit-fire eyes and a voice which, as the neighbours said, went through your head like a knife. The two had lived side by side in a pair of semi-detached cottages, like two matchboxes set end to end under one covering of thatch. The two front doors were but a foot or two apart and the best of good neighbours might have found such propinquity a strain on their neighbourly feelings. To Mrs. Pulbrook and Caroline it was fatal. Between their contests they were not on speaking terms and, after Mrs. Pulbrook had whitened her doorstep in the morning, her door was kept closed for the rest of the day, so that she might not see Caroline lounging on her own untidy doorstep and, as she said, be tempted to set the mark of her ten finger-nails on her impudent face.

F.T. from *Still Glides the Stream*

As is often the case with "Lammas Lambs" (late births), Peter was dearly loved by Flora and when he too was killed in action — his ship was torpedoed in mid-Atlantic in 1940 — she was so terribly distraught that she developed pneumonia, and during the remaining seven years of her life, when she should have been enjoying the growing acclaim for her literary works, she waned visibly and produced her final three volumes with a weary and heavy heart.

In a letter to Mr. Geoffrey Cumberlege, publisher to Oxford University, Flora wrote about Peter's death:

"It has been a great blow. I shall never forget that telegram. My boy was only 22, only two years out of his apprenticeship and just beginning to taste the sweetness of an independent life. He was our youngest, a late-comer and tenderly loved. That there are thousands of mothers and wives suffering as I am only seems to make it harder to bear. I mourn for them as well as for my own loss. His ship was carrying wheat, so innocently, when torpedoed . . . "

John Thompson had never accepted his wife as a writer in the early years and considered her literary efforts a waste of time, since the only money they had brought in so far had been spent by Flora on paying for a good private education for her children. In 1927 just after the family had settled into a new house in the country outside Liphook, called Woolmer Gate, John put in for promotion, much to his wife's dismay, and was posted to Dartmouth in Devon. Flora and the children stayed on for over a year at Liphook to sell the house before joining him, and they then moved into a secluded cottage overlooking the Dart estuary. It was here for the next 12 years that she put together the essays that eventually made up the book that was to launch her name so valiantly into the literary world.

Lark Rise was published first in 1939, but the war damped what would normally have been a singular success. Her second volume, *Over to Candleford*, appeared in 1941 although she had written it prior to Peter's death, and the third volume, *Candleford Green*, was published in 1943, the text often having been written, said Flora later, to the sound of falling bombs.

When John retired in 1940 the Thompsons moved to Brixham in south Devon. Their only remaining son, Basil, had emigrated to Australia and Winifred was a nurse in Bath. Encouraged by her publishers, the Oxford University Press, Flora forced herself to continue writing, and

Hips and Haws

On the following Sunday came the official "pig feast", when fathers and mothers, sisters and brothers, married children and grandchildren who lived within walking distance arrived to dinner. If the house had no oven, permission was obtained from an old couple in one of the thatched cottages to heat up the big bread-making oven in their wash-house. This was like a large cupboard with an iron door, lined with brick and going far back into the wall. Faggots of wood were lighted inside and the door was closed upon them until the oven was well heated. Then the ashes were swept out and baking-tins with joints of pork, potatoes, batter puddings, pork pies, and sometimes a cake or two, were popped inside and left to bake without further attention.

Meanwhile, at home, three or four different kinds of vegetables would be cooked, and always a meat pudding, made in a basin. No feast and few Sunday dinners were considered complete without that item, which was eaten alone, without vegetables, when a joint was to follow. On ordinary days the pudding would be a roly-poly containing fruit, currants, or jam; but it still appeared as a first course, the idea being that it took the edge off the appetite. At the pig feast there would be no sweet pudding, for that could be had any day, and who wanted sweet things when there was plenty of meat to be had!

But this glorious plenty only came once or at most twice a year, and there were all the other days to provide for. How was it done on ten shillings a week? Well, for one thing, food was much cheaper than it is today. Then, in addition to the bacon, all vegetables, including potatoes, were home-grown and grown in abundance. The men took great pride in their gardens and allotments and there was always competition amongst them as to who should have the earliest and choicest of each kind. Fat green peas, broad beans as big as a halfpenny, cauliflowers a child could make an armchair of, runner beans and cabbage and kale, all in their seasons went into the pot with the roly-poly and slip of bacon.

Then they ate plenty of green food, all home-grown and freshly pulled; lettuce and radishes and young onions with pearly heads and leaves like fine grass. A few slices of bread and home-made lard, flavoured with rosemary, and plenty of green food "went down good" as they used to say.

Bread had to be bought, and that was a heavy item, with so many growing children to be fed; but flour for the daily pudding and an occasional plain cake could be laid in for the winter without any cash outlay. After the harvest had been carried from the fields, the women and children swarmed over the stubble picking up the ears of wheat the horse-rake had missed. Gleaning, or "leazing", as it was called locally.

Up and down and over and over the stubble they hurried, backs bent, eyes on the ground, one hand outstretched to pick up the ears, the other resting on the small of the back with the "handful". When this had been completed, it was bound round with a wisp of straw and erected with others in a double rank, like the harvesters erected their sheaves in shocks, beside the leazer's water-can and dinner-basket. It was hard work, from as soon as possible after daybreak until nightfall, with only two short breaks for refreshment; but the single ears mounted, and a woman with four or five strong, well-disciplined children would carry a good load home on her head every night. And they enjoyed doing it, for it was pleasant in the fields under the pale blue August sky, with the clover springing green in the stubble and the hedges bright with hips and haws and feathery with traveller's joy . . .

FLORA THOMPSON

A row of former shipwrights' cottages at Buckler's Hard in Hampshire.

Home Thoughts
by FLORA THOMPSON

In Hampshire now, the woods are brown,
   The heath-sands tawny-gold with rain;
The mist lies blue on Bratley Down,
   The firelight flecks the window pane —
          In Hampshire now!

The wind comes screaming from the sea,
   The wild sea-horses champ and roar,
And every oak on Dudman's Lea
   Echoes the tumult of the shore —
          In Hampshire now!

The 'Wight lies wrapt in cloud and mist,
   Scarce once a week they'll see it clear,
And then it glows like amethyst —
   And Oh, I would that I were there,
          In Hampshire now!

Amidst the desert sand and heat,
   I hear the wheeling seabirds scream,
Scent the good smoke of burning peat,
   Then wake and find it but a dream —
          Ah, Hampshire dear!

The seaside resort of Brixham in Devon. The Thompsons moved there in 1940.

after the trilogy was published in 1945 they urged her to produce another book. This proved to be her last — *Still Glides the Stream* — which she finished only a few weeks before her sudden death, from heart failure, while alone in her room at Brixham, on 21st May, 1947. The book was published posthumously the following year.

Flora, whose death came as the world was beginning to awaken to her talents, had been received into the Roman Catholic church just before she died, and much to the surprise of her family. In a letter to H.J. Massingham, who wrote the introduction to her trilogy, she said:

> "Words as to the inner emotions do not come readily to me, for I have led an isolated life mentally and spiritually. The very people I know personally are not reading people and no-one but you has recognised my aims and intentions in writing of that more excellent way of life of our forefathers."

Flora Thompson has been loosely compared with three other great English women writers of the last century — Mary Russell Mitford, Mrs. Gaskell, and George Eliot. The first two, however, wrote of a cottage society far removed from the poverty of Lark Rise. Miss Mitford's village was like the lid of a chocolate box by comparison with the plain and uninspiring homes of Flora's birthplace, and Mrs. Gaskell's *Cranford* speaks of the genteel goings-on in a small township (Knutsford) rather than the authentic if crude ways of the Lark Rise commoners. Only George Eliot, who died at the height of her fame when

St. Valentine's Day

Upon St. Valentine's Day this year I found the first primroses. Just a crumpled rosette of soft green and three pale blooms; little enough in themselves, but how precious as a harbinger.

There was magic in them. All around was winter: the tiny plot between the mossed oak-roots where they grew was hard with frost, the dead leaves which sheltered them crisped with rime, and the sky between the bare boughs overhead glinted like steel. Even as I banked them round again a few icy splinters of hail edged in, but beneath the sheltering hedgerow those three pallid flowers had power to create a miniature spring.

Immediately to the inward eye sprang a vision of lanes and meadows starred with their fellows, of bluebell copses, June gardens and August poppy fields, of all the sweet pageant of which they were the earliest forerunners.

F.T. from "February" in *A Country Calendar*

"Queenie", the old lady who lived next door to Flora in Juniper Hill and who "told the bees" when her husband died.

Cars rush by the turning to Flora's "Lark Rise" on the A43 road between Oxford and Northampton.

Flora was a small child, revealed intimate glimpses of Victorian domesticity through actual experience in her native Warwickshire, but even these were of a higher social level, though still working class.

Flora Thompson was born at the beginning of what could be described as the greatest social upheaval in England, when the power of the squire and the rector began a rapid decline and the English peasantry emerged from ignorance and lost its bliss in the process. For despite their privations and penury the people were happy; Flora claimed in *Lark Rise*:

> Most of the men sang or whistled as they dug or hoed. There was a good deal of outdoor singing in those days. Workmen sang at their jobs; men with horses and carts sang on the roads; the baker, the miller's man, and the fish-hawker sang as they went from door to door; even the doctor and parson on their rounds hummed a tune between their teeth. People were poorer and had not the comforts, amusements or knowledge we have today; but they were happier. Which seems to suggest that happiness depends more upon the state of mind — and body, perhaps — than upon circumstances or events.

She developed that theme further in *Candleford Green*, claiming that every member of the community knew his or her place and few wished to change it:

> The poor, of course, wished for higher wages, the shopkeepers for larger shops and quicker turnovers, and the rich may have wished for higher rank and more extensive estates, but few wished to overstep the boundaries of class. Those at the top had no reason to wish for change and by others the social order was so generally accepted that there was no sense of injustice.
>
> The edifice of society as it then stood, apparently sound but already undermined, had served its purpose in the past. It could not survive in a changing world where machines were already doing what had been men's work, and what had formerly been the luxuries of the few were becoming the necessities of the many; but in its old age it had some pleasant aspects and not everything about it was despicable.

Today, the pilgrim to "Lark Rise" will find a Juniper Hill little changed from Flora's days . . . there are fewer cottages now, of course, and some have modern additions and television aerials aloft. But the "End House" is still there, blue-slated now instead of thatch, and has been renamed "Lark Rise". A plaque on the wall tells the curious that "Flora Thompson lived here". Next door is "Queenie's

76

Cottage", very little changed from the days when old Queenie, according to Flora, came out of her house to her beloved beehives to tell them of her husband's death, according to the old country custom of "telling the bees" of a calamity.

The lane that links the cottages in the Rise is still as it was, pot-holed and unmade, and the cornfields sweep almost up to the cottage doors. The *Fox* public house, called the "Waggon and Horses" in the book, is now being run by a Miss Jean Morris, whose family were landlords in Flora's day. Just over a mile down the narow country lane is the tiny village of Cottisford, called Fordlow in the book. The school that Flora attended is now a private house, but the church is unaltered — a brass plaque over the Timms's family pew records the deaths of the village boys in the Great War . . . and the name of Edwin Timms is at the bottom of the short list. From that pew Flora and Edwin looked out of the church door in summer at the birds and butterflies passing by, with only one eye and ear on the preacher.

In her short biography of Flora Thompson, published by John Murray, Margaret Lane says:

"What made her different from the other children who shared her experience, but who found nothing in them significant or remarkable, was her marvellously deep focus of observation. The annals of the poor are rarely written; they have no archives. Country churchyards are full of the bones of men and women who have lived her life and found nothing to say about it."

Much of the memorabilia of Flora Thompson — her scrap books, letters, and the script of a further autobiographical work entitled *Heatherley* which Flora did not consider worthy of publication, are no longer to be found in this country. They have been acquired by the University of Texas and form part of their literary museum and archives.

To commemorate her centenary in 1976, special exhibits were arranged at Banbury museum in Oxfordshire, and at the Selbourne Bookshop in Hampshire, but the greatest living testimony to the simple art of Flora Thompson is to be found in her trilogy *Lark Rise to Candleford*, which some now regard as an immensely readable social document. But to others it is the moving life-story of a lovable Oxfordshire village lass told with the honesty and vigour that can only stem from a deep love of the English countryside from whence she came.

Chronology of Flora Thompson

1876 Flora Timms (Laura of *Lark Rise*) born on December 5th at Juniper Hill, Oxfordshire.

1878 Edwin (Edmund in the book) her brother born at Juniper Hill.

1880 Starts school at Cottisford (Fordlow).

1887 Queen Victoria's Golden Jubilee: Village Feast.

1891 Leaves home to work in the Post Office at Fringford (Candleford Green).

1897 Moves to Grayshott (Surrey) to work as village postmistress.

1900 Meets and later marries John William Thompson, a post office clerk from Aldershot.

1901 Moves to Bournemouth, where two of her children, Winifred and Basil, are eventually born.

1912 Wins prize in "Literary Monthly" competition, and commences writing articles for various newspapers and magazines.

1916 Edwin, her beloved brother, killed in action in Belgium. Moves to Post Office at Liphook. Wins literary prize for essay on Jane Austen.

1918 Third child (Peter) born.

1921 Book of verse *Bog Myrtle and Peat* published — a commercial failure.

1924 She founds the Peverel Society, a postal association for literary aspirants.

1927 Thompson family moves house to Woolmer Gate, near Liphook.

1928 John Thompson promoted to postmaster of Dartmouth.

1929 Flora and children move to Dartmouth.

1931 Dr. Ronald Macfie, author and her "beloved friend", dies.

1937 Begins work on *Lark Rise*.

1939 *Lark Rise* first published.

1940 Peter, youngest son, killed in Merchant Navy — torpedoed in mid-Atlantic. John Thompson retires. He and Flora move to Brixham, Devon.

1941 *Over to Candleford* published.

1943 *Candleford Green* published.

1945 Trilogy *Lark Rise to Candleford* published.

1947 Dies at Brixham, May 21st. Buried at Dartmouth.

1948 *Still Glides the Stream* published posthumously.

FRANCIS BRETT YOUNG

(1884-1954)

The Worcestershire doctor who became a bestselling novelist

Church Bells

Their voices made an airy maze, soaring and wheeling dizzily above the steeple like swifts on a summer evening, while beneath them in the quivering heat-haze that wrapped the Severn Plain, the bells of other villages hummed, throbbed and trembled like a bourdon of bumble-bees in the lime-blossom.

F.B.Y. from *Portrait of Clare*

Between the wars one English novelist's name stood out more than almost any other on the bookshelves of home and library for his published works were not only prolific but they also spoke the language of the literary middle class. His books, largely of English village life, were avidly read by royalty and commoner alike, and some were later turned into successful films. Yet today, at a time when there is an outcry against the paucity of decent literature, when honest English fiction is threadbare of talent, few people have ever heard of, let alone read the delightful novels of . . . Francis Brett Young.

His triple name has an oddly American ring to it, but he was a full-blooded Englishman with an international reputation . . . yet, sadly, he could now well be called "Worcestershire's forgotten author".

Francis Brett Young was born at The Laurels, an ivy-clad Victorian villa on the edge of Halesowen, on a Sunday evening in June 1884, the eldest son of the town's much-respected doctor, Thomas Brett Young, and was baptised at the parish church with the slender spire where his father was churchwarden for many years. A plaque inside the church today records the belated and brief homage of his native town . . . but the church itself is now as much an oasis among a desert of architectural mediocrity as the writings of its famous son, whose Midland novels of delicate prose are crowded out of libraries by a morass of modern sensationalism and vulgarity.

To the north east of the town, and well within sight of it, lay the expanding "new" city of Birmingham, growing ever larger and richer on the crest of the booming Victorian

Francis Brett Young, the doctor-novelist who magnificently achieved his childhood ambition to become a poet and writer.

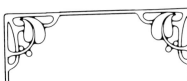

The Rain-bird

High on the tufted baobab-tree
Tonight a rain-bird sang to me
A simple song, of three notes only,
That made the wilderness more
    lonely;

For in my brain it echoed nearly
Old village church bells chiming
    clearly;
The sweet cracked bells, just out of
    tune,
Over the mowing grass in June —

Over the mowing grass, and
    meadows
Where the low sun casts long
    shadows,
And cuckoos call in the twilight
From elm to elm in level flight.

Now through the evening meadows
    move
Slow couples of young folk in love,
Who pause at every crooked stile
And kiss in the hawthorn's shade
    the while:

Like pale moths the summer frocks
Hover between the beds of phlox,
And old men, feeling it is late,
Cease their gossip at the gate,

Till deeper still the twilight grows,
And night blossometh like a rose
Full of love and sweet perfume,
Whose heart most tender stars
    illume.

Here the red sun sank like lead,
And the sky blackened overhead;
Only the locust chirped at me
From the shadowy baobab-tree.

F.B.Y.

The future novelist at the age of nine months with his mother.

machine age. But despite the proximity of this smoky giant of a neighbour, Halesowen managed to remain a country town when Francis was a boy, separated by a chasm of caste from the terraced sprawl of Birmingham — the "North Bromwich" of Brett Young's later novels.

Even in his boyhood years, Francis's heart and thoughts turned westward — to the lovely hills of Clent and Walton, the valleys of the Stour and Severn, then across the Teme to the forests and mountains of the Welsh Borders. And here, although perhaps unknown to him at the time, he shared an affinity with another English novelist whose name is deeply connected with the northern part of that region — Mary Webb of Shropshire. They were born in the same decade and both had their novels appreciated by the Prime Minister of the day, Stanley Baldwin. The Premier wrote to Francis Brett Young: "I am bearing *My*

Halesowen parish church where Francis was christened and where his father was a churchwarden.

Brother Jonathan off to Chequers for the weekend" and added that he hoped soon to "make the acquaintance of so distinguished a son of Worcestershire".

As a child Francis told his nanny he wanted to grow up to be a poet — and this he did, although after attending a mixed school at Sutton Coldfield, and later Epsom College, Surrey, he yearned to go to Balliol College, Oxford, but his father could not afford the fees. So instead he studied medicine at Birmingham University and became a doctor like his father.

If poetry was in his head, music was in his soul . . . implanted there by his mother, who played Mendelssohn and Beethoven to him as a child. His novels later confirmed his love of music, for many of them contain a character adept at the piano, as was his mother in real life, and he later said that beautiful music took him back to the garden of the family home at Halesowen, reminding him of the "scent of stocks and gillyflowers and lilac".

Francis was a romantic all his life, as any reader of his work can discern. When he was still a student, aged 20, he went to a college dance at Edgbaston (near the famous Test cricket ground) and met Jessica Hankinson from Alvechurch, also in Worcestershire. She was studying to become a Physical Training mistress. Both quickly discovered a mutual enjoyment in classical music and the joys

Francis Brett Young as a boy of four in his sailor suit.

81

Francis, pictured when he was a medical student, and Jessica with whom he fell in love and married.

Francis's father, Doctor Thomas Brett Young.

of the countryside, walking hand-in-hand through the hills and woodlands of Worcestershire.

Inevitably, they fell madly in love. Within a year he had proposed, but decided to wait before revealing their plans, knowing that their respective families would be shocked to hear of anything likely to distract from their studies. As it was the pair eventually eloped in December 1908 to avoid the fuss of a carefully planned "county" wedding, hurrying off to Somerset where they were married in a snowstorm. Much of the happiness they found in their marriage, which lasted until death parted them 46 years later, comes through the pages of Brett Young's novels. Theirs was an idyllic, old-fashioned love — sadly shadowed by a lack of children, but warmed by their many like interests, notably music. In her biography of her husband, written after his death, Jessica tells of a day in their courtship when they booked tickets for a concert at which Edward Elgar conducted his own composition *The Dream of Gerontius* in Worcester Cathedral . . . "in lovely autumn sunshine we entered the Cathedral spellbound with anticipation . . . and were completely overcome by the beauty of this immortal music".

After Brett Young had qualified he joined a merchant ship as a doctor, sailing to China and Japan, but his return to England in the spring so impressed him that he wrote: "I have just emerged from a dream . . . walking amidst the greenest of hedgerows told me a thousand times over that I was in my own England". The poetry and depth of feeling in the words he wrote presaged the talent for writing that was inside him, and after their secret marriage he took Jessica to Brixham in Devon where he had bought a small medical practice.

Worcester Cathedral, where on a memorable day Francis and Jessica witnessed Edward Elgar conducting his own music.

The Motor Car

That motor car was an offence to God and man, destroying the peace of every street it invaded with fumes of burnt oil and an exhaust that pounded like a water hammer.

If it were not over-lubricated it grew hot and gave up the ghost, its inadequate bearings threatening to seize. Its radiator which had to be filled up ten times a day, steamed like a samovar: you could have made tea from it at any moment. The ignition was supplied through a commutator to which short-circuits were second nature, from a wet — a too wet — battery, carried on the running board, that had to be recharged every fortnight. Its lion-hearted engine would "negotiate" (as the salesman put it) any ordinary hill, in time, with coaxing. Unfortunately some of the hills were extraordinary; the bottom gear was too high for them and I was forced to ascend them backwards in reverse.

F.B.Y. from *My Brother Jonathan*

In 1911, while the country was immersed in the celebrations for the coronation of King George V, the young doctor and his wife rushed back to the Border Country, starting a 175-mile walk from Ludlow in Shropshire through the Welsh Marches, staying in country inns overnight and sharing the simple fare of shepherds they met en route. It was following a similar walk, in which he came across the massive excavations for a reservoir in the Grwyne Valley to serve the needs of thirsty Birmingham, that he wrote his first book *Undergrowth* in collaboration with his younger brother Eric, published in 1913. It was also to inspire him later for one of his many best-sellers, *The House under the Water*, a copy of which he presented to the Queen in 1953.

Five Degrees South

I love all waves and lovely water in
    motion,
That wavering iris in comb of the
    blown spray:
These I have seen, these I have
    loved and known:
I have seen Jupiter, that great star,
    swinging
Like a ship's lantern, silent and
    alone
Within his sea of sky, and heard
    the singing
Of the south trade, that siren of the
    air,
Who shivers the taut shrouds, and
    singeth there.

                                    F.B.Y.

In the meantime, Jessica was establishing herself as an artist in her own right — as a singer she was in steady demand by Sir Henry Wood for his Promenade Concerts in London. She was also an accomplished pianist, and the Brett Youngs were noted among friends for their delightful musical evenings.

When the First World War broke out, Francis enlisted in the Medical Corps and served at first as officer in command of a field ambulance in German East Africa, where he suffered much from the heat and privation. His experiences there inspired much of his early poetry which was published by Martin Secker under the title of *Five Degrees South!*

At the same time he wrote his first successful prose work, *Marching on Tanga*, based on his experiences with General Smuts in East Africa. A review stated: "Not often has actual war been written in terms of artistic beauty". General Smuts told him that Kipling considered it one of the best three war books he had read.

After the war he returned to his medical practice in Brixham, but his disabilities soon prevented him continuing as a doctor and he began to write as a means of earning a living.

Recurrent migraine headaches affected Brett Young throughout his life, but it was the war that first exhausted him. This meant that he had to seek recuperation abroad in warmer climates. However, he made literary capital from these sojourns and met many of the most prominent men-of-letters with whom he made lasting friendships. In 1919 he and his wife bought a villa and went to live in Capri and there made the acquaintance of many sun-loving writers who, like himself, had not yet made their way to fame and affluence. D.H. Lawrence, Compton MacKenzie, and Norman Douglas of *South Wind* fame, were to be numbered among his friends.

Here Brett Young found great peace and contentment, in spite of the general opinion of the islanders that he must be mad to work and write instead of "just sitting in the sun". It was here that he wrote thirteen of his novels including *Portrait of Clare* regarded by many as his best and most English of novels. Young often referred to this work as "the dreadful, the enormous Midland novel". It gained him the James Tate Black Memorial Prize. Robert Church wrote of *The Portrait*: "The tale is plain and unadorned . . . as perfect a love-idyll as modern fiction

Francis Brett Young when he was in the army in Africa.

has given us". At this time *The Saturday Review*, that acme of critical perfection, wrote of Brett Young: "He handles language like a lover and can always imprison some aspect of truth in a single phrase. He has what few novelists possess, the gift of depicting men and women in relation to their livelihood."

In 1929 the Youngs returned to England and bought a house, Esthwaite Lodge, near Hawkshead, in the Lake District. It was here that he wrote *My Brother Jonathan* which was an immediate success. It sold more in three weeks in England than any of his earlier books in a year. As he himself said, it had taken fourteen years and fifteen books to reach this stage. He was invited to America to lecture, and distinguished people from the literary world all wished to meet him. He was invited to Max Gate, the home of Thomas Hardy, probably our most notable writer of the time: H.G. Wells, J.B. Priestley, Charles Morgan, Hugh Walpole and Bernard Shaw showered him with praise and welcomed his acquaintance.

He and his wife now decided to buy Craycombe House,

In Italy

It was evident that the whole village of Monfalcone had turned out to meet the Miss Isits. From the first moment when the cracks of the whip, the crunching of wheels and the clatter of hooves echoed through it, the little piazza had broken into life, like a kicked ant-heap. Scores of children, some of whom had obviously been put to bed, appeared from dark-arched alleys and danced about them; women suddenly thrust wide the windows of upper storeys and leant over on their balconies shouting to their neighbours below and on the opposite side of the square; shopkeepers and customers crowded the doors of groceries and vegetable shops; a squat round-spectacled clerical figure in a soutane emerged from the door of the church; from the steps of the town-hall two armed policemen in three-cornered hats and dark cloaks lined with scarlet descended, with the intention, as Miss Ellen thought, of protecting them from the crowd. They did nothing of the sort, but stood by, with superb indifference, while the remainder of the crowd pressed round them like bees swarming around a queen. Some of the bolder children pulled faces and others spat. One ragged boy would have clambered into the carriage had not Stewart leapt up snarling and showing his teeth.

"Inglese..." this horrid child bawled hoarsely. "Castello Inglese!"

"They evidently expect us and know who we are," Ellen thought, "but they're not very polite. Everybody seems to shout in Italy."

F.B.Y. from *A Man About the House*

Old Hammond

He wore a pepper and salt coat, full-skirted, of the kind that prosperous farmers use for riding, a folded Ascot cravat secured by a horse-shoe tiepin, and a tall square-topped felt hat which he neglected to remove. His clothes, indeed, seemed more suited to the practice of agriculture than that of mid-wifery; the black bag which he carried should have contained samples of oats rather than forceps. He stood there, a gaunt and grizzled figure, blinking at the light; the grey stubble on his lean jaw gave him a hungry wolfish look; but his features, though shrunken and discoloured by the changes of age, showed traces of the nobility which Jonathan had noticed in his daughter's. He had the same straight overheavy eyebrows, the same firm, yet potentially passionate mouth, though the lips were thinned by age and of a bluish pallor. His face was that of a man mortally tired, not only by conscious exertion but by the unconscious struggle of a strong spirit battling with age.

F.B.Y. from *My Brother Jonathan*

Esthwaite Lodge, where the novelist wrote My Brother Jonathan.

A corner of Hawkshead in the Lake District. The Youngs bought a house just outside the little Lancashire town, see the drawing opposite.

a mile out of the picture-book village of Fladbury in their native Worcestershire, which after renovation became their home for the next eleven years. The return to his beloved county was the inspiration for a number of his next novels, all written at Craycombe House. Among these were *White Ladies, Far Forest, Portrait of a Village, Dr. Bradley Remembers, The City of Gold,* and parts of his great poetic epic *The Island,* the story of England in verse. These were halcyon days when he gave large garden parties in Craycombe and spent many days at the county ground watching cricket for which game he had a great affection.

It was at Craycombe that the Brett Youngs entertained

Craycombe House near Fladbury in Worcestershire where many of his finest novels were written.

two of their dearest friends — John Masefield and his wife, Constance, with whom they shared a deep love of England and its flora and fauna.

In between bouts of illness, and the constant outpouring of novels which by now had a world-wide following, he loved fishing in the rivers of Worcestershire and Herefordshire. He also developed a keen interest in farming, planting plum orchards at Craycombe and breeding Wessex Saddleback sheep.

Worcestershire place names, though thinly disguised in his novels, are readily recognised by people of the county and round about. Halesowen became Halesby, Stourbridge was changed to Stourton, and his village of Chaddesbourne D'Abitot in *This Little World* was modelled on the Chaddesley Corbett of reality. His Monk's Norton, in *Portrait of a Village*, could apply to several Worcestershire villages like Abbot's Morton which is only a few miles from Craycombe, or Fladbury which is nearer still, but is in fact a composite of many such villages.

When the Second World War broke out in 1939 Francis immediately gave Craycombe House over to the Red Cross as a convalescent home for wounded soldiers and moved with his wife into the humble gardener's cottage on the estate. He volunteered for service "of a kind", but to his disappointment was never called upon. In 1941 he began writing *The Island*, an epic poem of England from prehistoric times right up to the Battle of Britain, hailed by critics

The Doctor

Sometimes he would come home with a small insect of some kind in a pillbox and arrange it under the microscope on the table under the dispensary window; and he'd say: "Wonderful . . . wonderful!" not because he'd made any biological observations, but just because it revealed a lot of unsuspected detail.

It was a favourite trick of his to show his patients a sample of their own blood corpuscles under the microscope too. "There they are," he'd say, "like a pile of golden guineas, and if you had a millionth part as many guineas as you have of these in your body, you'd be the richest man in England."

F.B.Y. from *The Young Physician*

The Worcestershire village of Fladbury.

A portrait of Francis Brett Young by Cathleen Mann.

as a gem of English literature when it was published in 1944.

By now their home in Capri was sold and the Brett Youngs, finding winter in Worcestershire too cold for his constitution, bought a house at Talland in Cornwall, but even this corner of England was a form of exile and when the spring broke they rushed back to their beloved Worcestershire.

In October 1944 Francis suffered a serious heart attack. Although he slowly recovered he remained a sick man and his doctor advised him to live abroad permanently — like a prison sentence to an Englishman. So once again, this time with deep sadness, he left England to sail to South Africa in the summer of 1945 as the bells of peace were ringing out all over the free world. He made a couple of sea trips back to England during the next few years, but his health continued to deteriorate and he died in a Cape Town nursing home in March 1954. In keeping with his dearest wish his widow brought his ashes back from South Africa to his beloved England, where they were placed in Worcester Cathedral beneath a plaque inscribed, simply: *Francis Brett Young — Physician, Poet, Novelist.*

How do we account for the indifference or lack of knowledge of today's reading public regarding Francis Brett Young? The first reason could well be the writer's style. It is lyrical in its beauty and few best-selling novelists today would claim that as an attribute. Life has changed in its

EASTER
by FRANCIS BRETT YOUNG

Photo: *Gathering spring flowers in the woods.*

Adown our lane at Eastertide
Hosts of dancing bluebells lay
In pools of light: and "Oh!" you cried,
"Look, look at them: I think that they
Are bluer than the laughing sea,"
And "Look!" you cried, "a piece of the sky
Has fallen down for you and me
To gaze upon and love," ... And I,
Seeing in your eyes the dancing blue
And in your heart the innocent birth
Of a pure delight, I knew, I knew
That heaven had fallen upon earth.

A RECOLLECTION

by C.P. SNOW

I first met Francis Brett Young in December 1938. I had gone down from Cambridge to Antibes for a holiday, the last holiday abroad, as we all guessed, for long enough. When I arrived at the hotel the proprietor told me that an English writer and his wife were staying there, and gave me their name. I knew the name already. All through the Thirties Brett Young had been one of the great popular successes. But until twenty-four hours before, however, I had not read a word he had written.

By a coincidence, a book of his, bound in the brown paper uniform of one of the old-fashioned Cambridge book clubs, had been dropped in my rooms just before I had set out. It was much better than I had somehow assumed, or been told. A good deal of it was romantic in a way I couldn't take: but nevertheless there was something interesting, flickering and shimmering just below the surface.

I looked forward to meeting him. Fairly soon, I realized that he was a most interesting man. In the book I had read, and in most of the others, the subtlety is evanescent; with the man himself, it was present all the time, tantalizing, probing, describing psychological manoeuvres, sometimes for sheer fun, sometimes out of obsessive curiosity. He was, in fact, one of the most subtle and complex characters I have known.

He looked, I often thought, like a colonial governor slightly down on his luck; not much like the GP he,

(continued on opposite page)

The novelist in 1927 . . . with a favourite pipe.

acceptance of what is readable. We have only to look at the covers of paperbacks on booksellers' shelves to see what sells today. Acceptable style now demands dramatic short-sentenced prose: otherwise the reader will never get beyond the first fifty lines.

Secondly, Brett Young in all his novels is ranged inalienably beside the Absolute Beauty in what he is disposed to feel is the last battle of her campaign with the "dirty devices of the world"; and his books all report typical incidents from the fighting. It is an ironical and an interrogating as well as a tragic mood, very like Hardy, but with the difference that the latter blamed external causes for his characters' fates, whereas Brett Young's characters are free from this and meet their fate in ordinary circumstances arising from their own environment. But do young people outside university courses ever read Hardy or concern themselves, however unconsciously, with the pursuit of Beauty?

Connected with the above is the author's puritan purpose. He never dealt with physical love outright, and never — except in a moralistic sense — brought it to bear on his characters. You may imagine how well that goes down with many modern readers!

Perhaps it is that Brett Young was so Victorian in style and outlook that he is no longer topical in the widest sense of the word. Perhaps it is because his later work did not

90

The peaceful interior of Worcester Cathedral, Francis Brett Young's final resting place.

keep up the expectations of the literary critics, who avowed for him total success. Although he was always a popular writer during his literary lifetime, and was greatly concerned with his annual sales, the real reason may be that the public has changed, and not the man.

But all wheels, even the literary one, turn full circle in time and perhaps as the world eventually rejects the permissiveness and profanity of the post-war years, so it will turn back to the purity and gentleness of country authors like Francis Brett Young.

(continued from opposite page)

following his father, had once been. The lids came down sadly over his eyes: but suddenly one was aware, beneath the lid, of a large violet eye, sly and mischievous, missing nothing. He was an extremely good mimic. There was a good deal of the actor about him — or rather of the actor-in-private. He showed all the contradictions of this kind of labile nature. I think he often found his temperament a good deal too complex to handle at all easily. He found it too complex also to express easily in books. He knew a great deal about people, and some of that comes through. But his writing is, most of it, less variegated than he was himself.

(from the Preface to Jessica Brett Young's biography of her husband published in 1962)

The Novels of Francis Brett Young

Undergrowth (1913); Deep Sea; The Dark Tower (1914); The Iron Age (1916); Marching on Tanga (1917); The Crescent Moon (1918); The Young Physician (1919); The Tragic Bride (1920); The Black Diamond; The Red Knight (1921); Pilgrim's Rest (1922); Woodsmoke; Cold Harbour (1924); Sea Horses (1925); Portrait of Clare (1927); The Key of Life; My Brother Jonathan (1928); Black Roses (1929); Jim Redlake (1930); Mr. and Mrs. Pennington (1931); The House under the Water; Blood Oranges (1932); The Cage Bird and other stories (1933); This Little World (1934); White Ladies (1935); Far Forest (1936); They Seek a Country; Portrait of a Village (1937); Dr. Bradley Remembers; The Christmas Box (1938); The City of Gold (1939); Mr. Lucton's Freedom; Cotswold Honey and other stories (1940); Man about the House (1942); In South Africa (1952); Wistanslow (1956).

JOHN OXENHAM

(1852-1941)

The businessman with a double identity

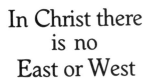

In Christ there is no East or West

In Christ there is no East or West,
In him no South or North,
But one great fellowship of love
Throughout the whole wide earth.

In him shall true hearts everywhere
Their high communion find,
His service is the golden cord
Close-binding all mankind.

Join hands, then, brothers of the
faith,
Whate'er your race may be!
Who serves my Father as a son
Is surely kin to me.

In Christ now meet both East and
West,
In him meet South and North,
All Christly souls are one in him,
Throughout the whole wide earth.

J.O.

If anyone had told Mr. William Dunkerley, a wholesale provision merchant of Manchester, that the son born to him in November 1852 would become a writer whose books, poems and hymns would be known and loved by people all over the world, he would have found it hard to believe, for he himself seemed to read only the Bible and the newspapers. The boy's name was William Arthur Dunkerley, but very few would know him as such for he adopted the pen-name of John Oxenham in 1896. To avoid confusion I shall refer to him as J.O.

The first step in his training as a novelist began at school with his love of history and it was continued when, after college, he went to France at the age of 19 to take charge of the Continental branch of his father's business. His time there did much more than give him an enjoyable life. It was the foundation of his career as a writer, for it gave him a thorough business training, and it was through the door of business that he later entered the literary world.

Developments in his father's trade, however, led to a complete change in his life when, in 1877, he and his young wife set off for America where a branch of the Dunkerley family business had opened in New York. But before long trouble hit the venture and it had to be adandoned. J.O. was loath to leave America, which he saw as a land of great opportunity, so he looked around for other work and decided to explore the possibilities of orange-growing in Florida and sheep farming in Georgia. Although he knew nothing of either trade, the prospect of a new and adventurous life attracted him so much that he set out full of hope and excitement.

John Oxenham in 1910. He wrote in a language and a style
that ordinary people could understand and enjoy.

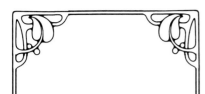

God's Sunshine

Never once since the world
 began
Has the sun ever once stopped
 shining.
His face very often we could not
 see,
And we grumbled at his
 inconstancy;
But the clouds were really to
 blame, not he,
For, behind them, he was
 shining.

And so — behind life's darkest
 clouds,
God's love is always shining.
We veil it at times with our
 faithless fears,
And darken our sight with our
 foolish tears,
But in time the atmosphere
 always clears,
For His love is always shining.
                                    J.O.

Manchester's mighty Town Hall. John Oxenham was born in the city in 1852.

Nothing came of the trip, however, and reluctantly he returned to England. He found it difficult to settle down and before long was seeking new experiences. While in America he had read and enjoyed the *Detroit Free Press* and he wrote to the Editor suggesting an English edition. The Editor replied that one of his staff, Robert Barr, had a similar idea and was even then on his way to England to look into the possibilities. Barr met J.O. and out of that meeting came the English edition which ran profitably for about eight years. It was a hazardous venture for neither of the two men knew anything about the intricacies of publishing, but they learned by experience and made a success of it, Barr acting as editor and J.O. as business manager. So successful were they, in fact, that they also launched *The Idler*, a monthly magazine, and later J.O. collaborated with Jerome K. Jerome, author of *Three Men in a Boat*, to produce a weekly paper *To-Day*. In each case J.O. directed the business side, leaving literary matters to Barr and Jerome.

It was at this time that J.O. began to try his own hand at writing. Reading one of the stories sent in to the magazine he thought to himself that he could write as well as that. He tried and found that a new and fascinating hobby had opened for him, and it was now that "John Oxenham" was born. He was convinced that Fleet Street would not take him seriously as an author if he wrote under the name of W.A. Dunkerley, the well-known business manager. So, for a time, the literary world knew both W.A. Dunkerley and John Oxenham, although the two were never connected and the latter was never seen. Editors found that they could not interview him, and even correspondence with him was a lengthy business. It was understood that he lived in Scotland and that he was frequently away on fishing trips! The real truth was that, to hide his identity, J.O. sent all his letters and messages from London to a sister-in-law in Greenock, and she repacked them and posted them to his agent in London. The agent replied to the Greenock address, and the letters were forwarded to J.O. in London. Years later John Oxenham was to become one of England's best-known and most prolific writers, with more than 40 novels and 30 other books to his credit, plus deeply-moving poetry, and was the author of the Great War's most popular hymn. But it was as the writer of a thriller serial which, in 1896, gave Londoners the jitters that he first achieved notoriety.

The serial was called *The Mystery of the Underground* and, for a writer ostensibly living somewhere in Scotland, it showed a remarkable insight into the daily workings of the London Tube system as well as the current thoughts of passengers who used it regularly. The articles centred around the theme that a murder took place on one of the Underground trains every Friday night. Published in the popular weekly magazine *To-Day*, the London public became so affected by the serial that many passengers refused to travel by Tube on a Friday night and London Transport eventually sent a formal letter of protest to the Editor of *To-Day*. He in turn hurried to discuss the matter with his firm's business manager, Mr. William Arthur Dunkerley, a former wholesale grocer from Manchester and the very model of a quiet and self-effacing English gentleman. It must have been a difficult conversation . . . for the sober-sided businessman was the holder of the secret. He was the mysterious John Oxenham, though no-one knew it. And even then he didn't reveal his identity. He persuaded his Editor that the Underground murder mysteries seemed likely to end soon. And so they did . . . John Oxenham brought the serial to a timely close.

THE WAYS

To every man there openeth
A Way, and Ways, and a Way.
And the High Soul climbs the
 High Way,
And the Low Soul gropes the Low,
And in between, on the misty flats,
The rest drift to and fro.
But to every man there openeth
A High Way, and a Low,
And every man decideth
The Way his soul shall go.

J.O.

What Can a Little Chap Do?

What can a little chap do
For his country and for you?
What can a little chap do?

He can play a straight game all
    through; —
That's one good thing he can do.

He can fight like a knight
For the Truth and the Right; —
That's another good thing he can do.

He can shun all that's mean,
He can keep himself clean,
Both without and within; —
That's a very fine thing he can do.

His soul he can brace
Against everything base,
And the trace will be seen
All his life in his face; —
That's an excellent thing he can do.

He can look to the light,
He can keep his thought white,
He can fight the great fight,
He can do with his might
What is good in God's sight; —
Those are truly great things
    he can do.

Though his years be but few,
If he keep himself true
He can march in the queue
Of the Good and the Great,
Who battled with Fate
And won through; —
That's a wonderful thing he can do.

And — in each little thing
He can follow the King,
Yes — in each smallest thing
He can follow the King, —
He can follow the Christ, the King.

J.O.

John Oxenham correcting proofs watched by his pet dog "Teufel".

This double identity led to one tantalising incident when J.O.'s own board of directors discussed the price to be paid for a John Oxenham short story and to his chagrin, as a member of the board, J.O. had to agree to a sum lower than he had hoped to receive! The irony of the incident lay in the fact that, as managing director, J.O. was constantly urging economy on the board, and so could hardly take the opposite line on this occasion.

Soon J.O. realised that he could not carry on the two jobs satisfactorily, and that he must choose between them. John Oxenham was becoming well-known as a writer, and he needed more time to develop all the possibilities opening before him. So in 1898 the business manager resigned, and W.A. Dunkerley disappeared from Fleet Street. But John Oxenham's name continued to be seen in most of the monthly magazines, and on the covers of two novels a year for many years.

Although he found great happiness in the actual writing, these were anxious years at his home, Woodfield House in Ealing. He wrote: "To become a successful writer a man needs not only to have the power to write, but much more the power to *wait*, and I am not sure that the latter is not the supreme test". There were tedious delays while editors and publishers made up their minds and a still longer delay while the accountants made up their books. J.O., with a young

The writer's Middlesex home, next to the Ealing Cricket Ground.

family of six, and with other responsibilities, could not afford to wait, and for many years he was haunted by the fear of financial failure. No wonder he wrote:

> *I had done my sums, and sums, and sums,*
> *Inside my aching head.*
> *I'd tried in vain to pierce the glooms*
> *That lay so thick ahead.*
> *But two and two will not make five,*
> *Nor will do when I'm dead.*

But — and this is the important point — the title of the poem which begins, "I faced a future all unknown", is *God is Good*. And his religion was his sheet-anchor all through life. Without that strong and firm faith he never could have fought his way through the difficulties of those early years. But his faith, his belief in himself, the unswerving confidence of his wife and the happy atmosphere of his family around him, carried him on, and in time John Oxenham secured an established place in the literary world.

The eldest of that family of six, Elsie Jeannette, also adopted the surname Oxenham for her literary career and published 87 books between 1907 and 1959. Her "Abbey School" series were particularly popular among schoolgirls and are still in great demand today. The youngest daughter, Erica, wrote several novels but latterly saw herself mainly as J.O.'s business manager and companion and, towards the end of his life, as his collaborator in several

BIRTHDAY

Another milestone passed
And that much nearer is my
    journey's end, —
That end which is for me
But a beginning — *the* beginning.
And as I stand here
High on the crest of the hill,
And look back
Upon the long long winding track,
I marvel and give thanks,
For cheer, and comfort, and safe
    guidance,
Through those winding ways, —
Wild wanderings, and clouded
    days . . .

J.O.

The Novels of John Oxenham

God's Prisoner
Rising Fortunes
Our Lady of Deliverance
A Princess of Vascovy
John of Gerisau
Under the Iron Flail
Bondman Free
Mr. Joseph Scorer
Barbe of Grand Bayou
A Weaver of Webs
Hearts in Exile
The Gate of the Desert
White Fire
Giant Circumstance
Profit and Loss
The Long Road
Carette of Sark
Pearl of Pearl Island
The Song of Hyacinth
My Lady of Shadows
Great-Heart Gillian
A Maid of the Silver Sea
Lauristons
The Coil of Carne
Their High Adventure
Queen of the Guarded Mounts
Mr. Cherry Retired?!
The Quest of the Golden Rose
Mary All Alone
Red Wrath
Maid of the Mist
Broken Shackles
Flower of the Dust
My Lady of the Moor
"1914"
The Loosing of the Lion's Whelps
Corner Island
A Hazard in the Blue
The Perilous Lovers
Chaperon to Cupid
Scala Sancta
The Recollections of Roderic Fyfe
The Hawk of Como
Lake of Dreams

J.O.'s pen-name was adopted by other members of his family, seen together in this group picture taken at Woodfield House, Ealing, in 1920. Elsie (top left) used her father's surname-de-plume for all her 87 books — schoolgirl novels which are eagerly collected today. His youngest daughter Erica (bottom right) did the same, writing several novels and two biographical works of her father. Roderic (seated second left) wrote several books and became a clergyman; Hugo (seated right) was a newspaper editor; the two other girls, Theo (seated, far left) and Maida, helped at home.

books. The eldest boy, Roderic, became a Congregational minister and wrote several books for children as well as a dozen theological works, the best known perhaps being *Beyond the Gospels* published by Pelican. The two middle girls, Maida and Theo, were housekeepers, friends, and helpers to the busy household, particularly after their mother died in 1925. Hugo, the youngest, became a pilot in the Royal Flying Corps during the First World War, but obviously had journalism in his blood and went to East Africa where he became editor of *The Mombasa Times*.

John Oxenham the novelist was now successfully launched on his career, but all the time still another identity was quietly building itself up in the background. This was John Oxenham the poet or, as he put it, John Oxenham the writer of verses, for he was always modest about his poems.

From time to time for many years, verses had formed themselves in his brain, and he had casually noted them down. It was a collection of these verses which appeared in 1913 in a little book called *Bees in Amber*. His publishers, horrified that a well-known novelist should suddenly turn to writing poetry, refused the book. Whereupon, J.O. undertook the cost of production himself, and they reluctantly agreed to publish it, but urged him to print only 200. J.O. ordered 1,000! To their great surprise it was warmly welcomed and, with the outbreak of the First World War, the book soon became an outstanding success. It appealed both to the men at the Front and to their friends and relatives left lonely at home, with the result that, by the end of the war, 228,000 copies had been sold!

John Oxenham's success as a writer of verses came because he wrote as an everyday man, and so all men listened to him. He spoke from the heart and his verses are like himself — simple, unpretentious and deeply rooted in the things of the spirit. This common touch is perfectly exemplified in his beautiful *Little Te Deum of the Commonplace.*

> *For things unnumbered that we take of right,*
> *And value first when first they are withheld;*
> *For light and air; sweet sense of sound and smell;*
> *For ears to hear the heavenly harmonies;*
> *For eyes to see the unseen in the seen;*
> *For vision of The Worker in the work;*
> *For hearts to apprehend Thee everywhere; —*
>
> > *We thank Thee, Lord!*

> *For all life's beauties and their beauteous growth;*
> *For Nature's laws and Thy rich providence;*
> *For all Thy perfect processes of life;*
> *For the minute perfection of Thy work,*
> *Seen and unseen, in each remotest part;*
> *For faith, and works, and gentle charity;*
> *For all that makes for quiet in the world;*
> *For all that lifts man from his common rut;*
> *For all that knits the silken bond of peace;*
> *For all that lifts the fringes of the night,*
> *And lights the darkened corners of the earth;*
> *For every broken gate and sundered bar;*
> *For every wide flung window of the soul;*
> *For that Thou bearest all that Thou has made; —*
>
> > *We thank Thee, Lord!*

Many people wrote to him for help and advice or encouragement, and in his replies he always emphasised the idea that there must be the urge to write, whether novels or verses, or the work would not be worth the doing. He encouraged aspiring authors who had that urge, but was dissuasive toward dilettante ones. To one he wrote:

> *Write if you must,*
> *But — think on this —*
> *Christ wrote but once*
> *And then in dust.*

After the First World War J.O.'s career took a new turn. Just as the business man was superseded by the novelist, and the novelist by the poet, so now the poet gave place to

Other Works of John Oxenham

Bees in Amber (*305 thousand*)
"All's Well!" (*203 thousand*)
The King's High Way (*102 thousand*)
The Vision Splendid (*100 thousand*)
The Fiery Cross (*80 thousand*)
High Altars (*40 thousand*)
Hearts Courageous (*42 thousand*)
"All Clear!" (*25 thousand*)
The Hidden Years (*83 thousand*)
A Little Te Deum (*283 thousand*)
The Later Te Deums (*120 thousand*)
The Sacraments (*88 thousand*)
Wide Horizons (*20 thousand*)
Hymn for the Men at the Front
Chaos — and the Way Out
"Gentlemen — The King!"
The Wonder of Lourdes
The Cedar Box
Selected Poems
Winds of the Dawn (*Essays*)
The Man who Would Save the World
God's Candle
The Splendour of the Dawn
Cross Roads
A Saint in the Making
Anno Domini
God and Lady Margaret
Christ and the Third Wise Man
Out of the Body

Adieu and Au Revoir

by JOHN OXENHAM

As you love me, let there be
No mourning when I go, —
No tearful eyes,
No hopeless sighs,
No woe, — nor even sadness!
Indeed I would not have you sad,
For I myself shall be full glad,
With the high triumphant gladness
Of a soul made free
Of God's sweet liberty.

— No windows darkened;
For my own
Will be flung wide, as ne'er before,
To catch the radiant inpour
Of Love that shall in full atone
For all the ills that I have done;
And the good things left undone;
— No voices hushed;
My own, full flushed
With an immortal hope, will rise
In ecstasies of new-born bliss
And joyful melodies.

Rather, of your sweet courtesy,
Rejoice with me
At my soul's loosing from captivity.
Wish me "Bon voyage!"
As you do a friend
Whose joyful visit finds its happy end.
And bid me both "A Dieu!"
And "Au revoir!"
Since, though I come no more,
I shall be waiting there to greet you,
At His door.

And, as the feet of the bearers tread
The ways I trod,
Think not of me as dead,
But rather —
"Happy, thrice happy, he whose course is sped!
He has gone home — to God,
His Father!"

Covers of a couple of John Oxenham's novels.

the writer of religious books. Although aged 70, J.O. embarked on the most important phase of his literary work. All his life he had talked of writing a life of Jesus and when an American friend turned J.O.'s thoughts again in that direction he started on it once more with zest, and this time the story "just flowed out". "The story wrote itself", he said. "I simply acted as scribe putting it down on paper as it came". It was published in 1925 under the title of *The Hidden Years*. The *New York Sun* in a review said: "There are consummate works of art that appear just to have happened. This is one of them."

The Hidden Years was followed by other books dealing with the life of Christ and with the work of the apostles after Pentecost. They, too, found an appreciative and grateful public.

One would have expected that after a busy, energetic life, the advancing years would have irked him, and that he would have found life dull and tedious. But he did not. He had the capacity to adapt himself readily to new places and new conditions and in 1938, when a severe attack of bronchitis warned him that his travelling days were over, he settled down with great happiness in a small bungalow, "Conifers", up on the South Downs at High Salvington, near Worthing in Sussex, overlooking the sea. There he

Some Day . . .

Some day my little bark will touch
An unknown shore,
And I shall hear
A soft voice calling me by name,
And a strong hand will be
    outreached
To me, and I shall land without a
    fear,
For I have heard that voice before,
And it is dear to me.
So I shall step from out my useless
    bark
Into the eternal freshness
Of the morning Land
Where the New Day reigns
    eternally.

                J.O.

Memories of
'Granpa J.O.'

My grandfather, John Oxenham, was always a remote figure to me. I was 14 years old when he died and I saw him rarely, but I was aware of his existence from a very early age. From almost as long ago as I can remember I had heard of this mystical figure, "Granpa J.O." spoken of in tones of respect and affection somewhat akin to awe.

As I grew older I, too, viewed him in much the same light. This was partly due to the early conditioning and partly to the fact that I was gradually becoming aware that he was the author of many books, the more bloodthirsty of which, like *John of Gerisau, The Hawk of Como,* and *Under the Iron Flail,* I was already enjoying. Writing, too, was a trade to which I had begun to aspire. And, if I were to be completely honest, I would have to admit that part of the respect, affection and awe in which I then held Granpa J.O. was due to the fact that a Postal Order for 7s 6d arrived regularly from him on birthdays and at Christmas, when the going-rate among friends was only half-a-crown!

The occasions when we did meet, and which I can remember, were on family summer holidays from Birmingham to the sea, where J.O. lived in a large house in Worthing with his daughters. We saw little of the great man on these occasions but I remember that we were always having to be quiet because, we were told, "Granpa J.O. is writing".

It was on one of these visits, when I was about 10 years old, that I learned to swim. J.O., on hearing of these first floundering attempts, offered me 10 shillings when I could swim from one groyne to the next, non-stop, no touching. I practised hard until, by the end of the holiday, I was ready for the attempt. I made it, but with only my younger brother, Gregor, watching, and I was deeply impressed when no proof was requested, no adult witnesses required and the 10 shillings was handed over with congratulations and a shaken hand.

Later, when Granpa J.O. moved to the bungalow, "Conifers", up on the Downs at High Salvington, we went up for short visits from the big house. I was 14 and very much aware, on its merits, of the old man's literary reputation. I looked at him then with a respect and admiration for his books, his poems and his example, which feelings have in no way been dimmed by the years.

My aunt, Elsie Jeannette Oxenham, was living at the big house in Worthing when we made those summer visits. She was an even more remote figure than my grandfather, and an added reason for silence: "Aunt Elsie is correcting proofs!", we were told with finger to lips. We didn't know what it meant, but we tip-toed anyway. She appeared for dinner every evening and once, memorably, stayed afterwards to play games with us all, of the sitting-quietly variety. I remember the occasion particularly well for I lost at "Lexicon", a game at which I was normally very good, because I was afraid to put words on the table in case I spelt them wrongly in front of the authoress of so many books! Although written primarily for girls, I read — and have read since — enough of those books to understand their popularity then as well the renewed and increasing interest and demand for them now.

DESMOND DUNKERLEY

102

J.O. always had an affection for dogs (see poem on this page) like this one which he encountered whilst on holiday in the French Alps.

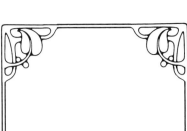

DOG FRIENDS

*Every dog I meet I like to greet
With a chirp and a cheerful word,
And each one throws me a grateful
    look,
And a joyful wag of the tail.
And he says, as plain as plain can
    be,
"Thank you, Man, for your
    thought of me."
And we each pass on the happier,
For the word and the wag of the
    tail.*

*And often in this perplexing life
When things seem all ajee,
God sends me a word of cheer and
    hope,
And I lift Him a glance of gratitude,
And pass with a wag of my tail,
As grateful to Him for the word of
    cheer,
As the little dog is to me.*

*And of these meetings there is no
    end
For I look on every dog as a friend.*

                  J.O.

was content to sit back and rest, knowing that he had done his best. He had lived a full and busy life. He had published 44 wholesome novels, 10 books of memorable verse and an even greater number of books on religious themes. Now, appreciating the fact that the bustle and battle of life were nearly over for him, he wrote:

> *By God's good Grace
> My race I ran,
> And now lie here
> A Grateful Man.*

But those last years were not idle ones. Two books appeared in 1940 and he was busy on another until three days before he died in January 1941. That was how he had always hoped it would be; he had always dreaded the thought of being past work.

> *Lord, when Thou seest that my work is done,
> Let me not linger on,
> With failing powers,
> Adown the weary hours, —
> A workless worker in a world of work.
> But, with a word,
> Just bid me home,
> And I will come
> Right gladly, —
> Yea, right gladly
> Will I come.*

Among the many notes found later was this one:

> "Thanks be to God for a life full-packed, with things that matter crying to be done — a life, thank God, of never-ending strife against odds . . . Just time enough to do one's best, and then pass on, leaving the rest to Him . . . "

SHEILA KAYE-SMITH

(1887-1956)

Storyteller of the Sussex Weald

It was the first 12 years of my life that made me a Sussex novelist. I still write, I know, from the impressions of those early days — pictures that I have always seen in a clear sunshine, vivid, slight, and sharp as swords in my memory. In a sense every farm I write of is Platnix Farm, and every human being is one or another of the people that I met there. My very earliest imagination was captured by the countryside that holds it still. S.K.-S.

A slender Edwardian schoolgirl sat in a pill-box brougham outside her home in St. Leonards-on-Sea, Sussex, patiently waiting for her father, the local doctor, to emerge with his little black bag. He had been called out in the gathering dusk to attend an urgent case in the village of Westfield, five miles away, and an invitation to accompany him on such a journey into the countryside she loved was too big a temptation to be missed.

She was 15 and, by her own admission, rather plain-looking with her hair skinned tightly back from her brows and stubby pig-tails poking out from her sailor hat, part of the uniform of the Hastings Ladies College at the turn of the century.

As they drove through the narrow, twisting Sussex lanes by the flickering light of leathern coach lamps, the girl breathed her native air and solemnly made three fervent vows for her future — one day she would become a celebrated author; secondly, and despite the muted disapproval of her parents, she would be "very High Church"; thirdly, she would live in her very own house in the countryside she was now riding through.

All three wishes came true for the doctor's determined daughter — Sheila Kaye-Smith, whose name and novels eventually became synonymous with the Sussex Weald. Her knowledge and love of this part of East Sussex and the Kentish borderland sparkled through the pages of dozens of her novels between the wars, until the villages and rolling heath and farmlands in this quiet corner of England became known as "Sheila Kaye-Smith Country".

The Weald itself stretches from Midhurst in the west to

Sheila Kaye-Smith, the doctor's daughter from St. Leonards-on-Sea who became the Storyteller of the Sussex Weald.

The Optimist

The earth is green, the earth is wide,
And when its widest bound is past,
There are the stars on every side,
For soaring souls to win at last —
There is no bound for those that fly,
Floorless and roofless is the sky,
Hope knows no hindrance but clipped
    wings,
So, throughout all life's little while,
My heart is happy, and I smile,
In spite of many things,
In spite of pain,
   In spite of fears,
    In spite of want,
     In spite of tears
      — In spite of you.

Mine is the future, and the past,
The growing and the dying gleam,
Mine is ambition till the last,
And there are dreams for me to dream.
Mine is the sagging Winter day,
Mine too the softness of the May,
The lusty strength of bread and wine,
The valiant dawn, the pondering night,
The flowering change from dark to light,
All holy things are mine,
In spite of pain,
   In spite of fears,
    In spite of want,
     In spite of tears
      — In spite of you.

Adventure weaves the shining dress
Experience at last shall wear,
Grief, rapture, triumph, bitterness
Combine to trace the pattern there.
All sorrow that my soul assails
Helps to embroider golden veils
To deck me in the glorious day
When I shall reign in endless rest,
So strength and laughter fill my breast,
And on my heartstrings play,
In spite of pain,
   In spite of fears,
    In spite of want,
     In spite of tears
      — In spite of you.

               S.K-S

A lovely childhood portrait of Sheila and her younger sister Mona.

Ashford (Kent) in the east, from Sevenoaks in the north, to Lewes and Rye in the south. But a more definitive area of "Sheila Kaye-Smith Country" lies roughly between Heathfield and St. Leonards in the west, and Cranbrook to Dungeness in the east — about a hundred square miles. When the local government authorities divided Sussex into two counties, East and West, in 1865 they did little more than follow the cultural and historical boundary . . . for the two "halves" have quite separate identities. The dialects, the landscape, the outlook of the people were, and in some cases still are, quite different. But whereas Hilaire Belloc would wander freely between the two in search of his inspiration, Sheila Kaye-Smith never strayed into the western territory, although she did include parts of south Kent in her stories.

She was born at Hastings on 4th February, 1887, the elder of two daughters. A shy and sensitive child, she preferred long, meandering walks in the countryside north of Hastings to the dubious pleasures of life in a seaside town. She explored the local area on foot, cycle and horseback, losing no opportunity to delve into the legends and lore of old Sussex.

She would watch the carriers' carts rolling out of Hastings in slow procession, trundling to the outlying villages and hamlets in the country she loved so dearly but could only visit in non-school hours. Once, after a day tramping in the fields and farms, she jumped on the back of a cart, legs dangling, and rode as a stowaway all the way back to

The historic town of Hastings where Sheila was born in 1887.

town . . . aged 18, and a straw-boatered Edwardian young lady in a long skirt!

She studied the dialect and the customs, often visiting remote farms and churches, and then returned to the privacy of her bedroom where, using school notebooks, she began secretly writing her first novels. By the time she left school at 17 she had already written thirteen, none of which had been read by anyone but herself. Indeed it was not until 1908 that she wrote her first novel for publication.

She purchased ten exercise books, then costing only a penny each, and by candlelight wrote the story of an itinerant preacher. Titled *The Tramping Methodist*, it took her a full year to complete. She borrowed £3.12s.6d. from her parents to have it re-typed from her pencilled script, and then sent if off to a London publisher. Seven anxious months later it appeared in print, and although it only brought her around £20 in royalties it put her name modestly into the literary world.

Local fame quickly followed for the 21-year-old girl, and Hastings opinion was that she was a thoroughly modern miss and probably even "one of those dreadful Suffragettes". Neither was remotely true, but when the house of the Hastings MP was burned down, local gossips pointed the finger of suspicion firmly at Sheila. Some overimaginative ones even claimed to have seen her set fire to it

Dedication

When Mass is said,
The music dead,
And the last lights upon the
    Altar-throne
Drop slowly one by one into the
    dark,
To the east
Turns the Priest,
And bows his knee before the
    sacred Ark
And whispers the Last Gospel
    through — alone.

So do I
When dreams die
And love's last wretched candle-
    lights are seen
Darkening upon the Altar of your
    heart,
Face the east,
And like the Priest
Say my Last Gospel through ere I
    depart,
And before leaving bow to
    What Has Been.

                       S.K-S.

Bride's Song

It was not always thus I loved,
Once, long ago, another love was
    mine,
A love that through the
    constellations moved
On fiery way divine —
It was not always thus I loved.

But can a bird for ever fly?
Too rare, too lofty, is the sky,
The poor bird folds his tired wings,
And in the tree-top sings,
And tries
To forget the skies.

It was not always thus I dreamed
Once, long ago, I walked in Paradise,
And through the coolness of the
    garden gleamed
An angel's beckoning eyes —
It was not always thus I dreamed.

But can the sun be ever bright?
He faints before the sword of night,
And back into the house we hie,
And with a candle try,
When day's done,
To forget the sun.

I went into the sunset, and I heard
Among the trees the faint note of a
    bird.

                        S.K.-S.

Beckley, one of the pretty Sussex villages lying at the heart of "Sheila Kaye-Smith Country".

while shouting "Votes for Women!" . . . but the shy young novelist was at home asleep in bed all the time. Even so, it took several years before the malicious rumour was eventually scotched.

So securely sheltered was her home-life that at 24 she looked only 19 and felt no more than 16 in experience, confessing to friends that she had "never been kissed". Readers of her early novels would have found this difficult to believe.

In 1909 her second novel, *Starbrace*, was published. It suffered similar low sales to the first, and her literary agent suggested Sheila needed to gain more experience of life, which meant emerging from the ordered calm of her Sussex home. She spent some weeks in London, visiting the house of the celebrated poet and authoress, Alice Meynell, and in 1910 went to Paris to broaden her knowledge of people, but while there fell victim to pneumonia and almost died. Only after a period of six months' convalescence in Sussex was she able to recommence writing again. Three more books came out before the First World War, but it was not until 1916 that her work leapt into the literary headlines with her sixth novel, *Sussex Gorse*, the story of a stubborn farmer's fight to tame a wild area of heathland.

Wartime England was a difficult environment for an aspiring young female author and in between making bandages for the troops, serving tea and buns in an Army canteen, and "adding to the muddle" of a War Office department as a clerk, she began writing the book which she always regarded as her best — *Little England.* This was a war book and the one novel in her arsenal of stories which she felt had never been fully appreciated at the time of its publication. But although the critics slammed it for dealing with "commonplace people", its low sales were probably due to its untimely appearance, just before the Armistice in 1918.

With peace came a great public rejection of war books in a general and natural desire to return to normal life. Even so, Sheila Kaye-Smith was well on the way to fulfilling her first schoolgirl wish, and in the first four years after the war came a dramatic upturn in her fortunes due to a trio of highly successful Sussex novels — *Tamarisk Town*, a story of Hastings which became a near bestseller, *Green Apple Harvest* and, most famous of all, *Joanna Godden*, the story of a strong-minded woman farmer on Romney Marsh, which sold 10,000 copies when it was first published in the autumn of 1921. Some years later the book was turned into a film starring Googie Withers in the title part.

When her next book, *The End of the House of Alard,* topped 40,000 copies, she could certainly claim to have made her mark on the literary scene. She now had more money than she knew what to do with and no longer had to make her own clothes — a process which, for her, had previously meant lying down full stretch on top of a length of dress material spread upon the floor, and then cutting round her body's shape with a pair of nail scissors!

"Happy ever after" novels were just going out of fashion when she reached the peak of her popularity between the wars, and marriage often began instead of finishing the story. Soon, literary tastes appeared at first sight to turn full circle with "boy meets girl" themes again . . . but this time the difference was that both of them were already married and the new novels centred themselves as much on getting rid of the old partnership as getting on with the new. In this regard, Sheila Kaye-Smith was a rebel. Although never a prude — how could she be when filling her novels with the rough-and-ready characters of the Sussex countryside? — she developed a winning style of dealing with real people without offending her deeply-held principles.

In 1914 she spent a time in Cornwall mixing with a

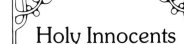

Holy Innocents

Today I keep a feast, with red and
  white —
The red blood and the snow-white
  innocence
Of little souls who had their recompense
Before they learned the horrors of the
  fight.

I see them running in their gardens gay,
They snatch the colours of the rainbow's
  flame,
And throw the stars about in childish
  game,
And pull the clouds to pieces for their
  play.

But these are not the throng the king did
  slay,
The babes for whom dark Rachael's
  head is bowed —
'Tis not for them her wailing rings so loud;
Other and holier Innocents are they.

These are the little ones who never
  wrought
Love's royalest wonder in a mother's eyes,
Who never brought a tender warm
  surprise
With groping lips to breasts till then
  unsought.

These are the fruit of hundredfold desires,
Ten thousand dreams begot this laughing
  band,
They fill the cities of a promised land —
Long promised, but not given — lost in
  fires.

These are the children I had hoped to
  show
The secret of this life, and all its love —
But they are playing with my dreams
  above,
While I plunge on through my dead
  hopes below.

Saved — Oh, perhaps from much that I
  must brave —
I worship you, sweet saints! — oh, pray
  for me!
The little children that shall never be —
The little children I shall never have.
                                    S.K.-S.

Sheila and her husband, the
Reverend T. Penrose Fry.

East Cliff, Hastings.

colony of authors — Hugh Walpole, Compton Mackenzie, J.D. Beresford, Dorothy Richardson and C.A. Dawson-Scott — in a tiny coastguard's cottage at St. Merryn, but remained largely unimpressed by them. She met Mary Webb — "a shy and timid person" — who was to Shropshire what Sheila was to Sussex (see separate chapter). Among other of her literary contemporaries was the ageing Thomas Hardy who invited her to his Dorset home, Max Gate, in 1920 soon after she had published *Green Apple Harvest*. They discussed their respective parishes — Hardy's Wessex and Sheila's Sussex — and the great man jokingly warned the budding novelist not to venture further west than the Isle of Wight! She also met, and disliked, D.H. Lawrence whom she described as "uncouth . . . a tangle of ideals and prejudices". But she got on famously with his charming wife.

Almost all of Sheila Kaye-Smith's novels reflected varying aspects of her interest in religion, and a few years after fulfilling her third wish by joining the "high" wing of the Church of England during the autumn of 1918, she found herself catapulted to the forefront of the Anglo-Catholic movement in the country, which was then smarting from the loss of G.K. Chesterton who had recently "gone over" to Rome. Sheila was a frequent speaker at High Church meetings, but in 1924 at the age of 37 she shocked the movement by marrying a curate — the Reverend Theodore Penrose Fry — for diehard Anglo-Catholics of the time subscribed to the view that their clergy should remain celibate.

Before meeting her husband she had been commissioned to write a series of articles on marriage and family life, but in the writing she realised how selfish and sterile her own life seemed, so she decided there and then upon a curious adventure, one which could have led to personal disaster but which, in fact, turned the course of her life.

She felt that spinsterhood was not for her, and yet she knew of no male acquaintance with whom she could even remotely fall in love. So, in her own words, unless she was to end up "utterly withered as a human" she decided in cold blood to marry the first man who asked her — whether in love or not — with the only proviso that she should like and respect him. When she met the unassuming Mr. Fry — son of a baronet (Sir John Fry) — and a curate at St. Leonards, Sussex, she agreed to his eventual proposal with eyebrow-raising alacrity . . . but despite the deep misgivings of

The taproom of a typical country pub where a game of dominoes can be a serious business . . .

Theology at the George

by SHEILA KAYE-SMITH

In the next waarld there ain't no inn —
That's what our Parson says —
Lik the old George down Brownbread Street;
My Lord! it 'ud be hard to beat,
Even up Lunnon ways.
There ain't one lik it in the town;
The ale is fine there, wood-nut brown,
Wud froth all stiff against your teeth.
Oh, the good stuff that's underneath!
Oh, the white gin! Oh, the black porter!
But Parson says in heaven there's water,

Milk and honey — teetotal muck!
And all the angels is temp'rance struck,
So's you cud roam from star to star
And never come on a licensed bar.
And as fur hell, down there they say
Your tongue's swelled out all black and thick
As a blood pudden, and Old Nick
Don't even allow a cup of tay . . .

So this is my advice, my lad —
Drink all the stuff that's to be had,
Brandy an' gin an' beer an' sherry;
Smoke yer pipe, spit and be merry,
Drink while you can, for when life's o'er,
You'll have to be sober for ever more.

Sheila Kaye-Smith enjoys a moment of refreshing relaxation at her home in Little Doucegrove near Brede, Sussex.

A FARMER'S PHILOSOPHY

In her novel *Sussex Gorse*, published in 1916, Sheila Kaye-Smith tells of the pressures within a farming family, struggling to make ends meet in difficult times. Farmer Joseph Backfield tells his two sons this recipe for happiness, born out of a lifetime's experience:

"I've no ambitions, so I'm a happy man. I doan't want nothing I haven't got, and so I haven't got nothing I doan't want."

some of her London literary friends, the marriage lasted more than 30 years "without a single regret".

The newly-weds moved to Notting Dale, where Mr. Fry was given a High Church curacy, and Sheila embraced the gruelling life of a clergyman's wife in one of London's seamier quarters. But she still found time to write, and a spate of books followed including *Saints in Sussex* (1926), a volume of her poems, plus two mystery plays in which she attempted to stage the Gospel stories of the Nativity and the Passion in the setting of the Sussex countryside and the dialect of its farming folk.

When her husband was moved to a more fashionable parish in South Kensington, with its fine building and affluent congregation, Sheila soon discovered that too much magnificence unbalanced her faith. Her feelings were revealed in her next novel *Shepherds in Sackcloth*, which told the story of a Church of England clergyman and his wife struggling on a meagre income to run a parish and fulfil Christ's mission.

By the time this novel appeared Sheila was about to accomplish her third wish . . . but not before she had shocked her contemporaries yet again. In 1929, just before Christmas, she and her Anglican priest-husband were converted to the Roman Catholic faith and, partly to flee from the inevitable publicity but also to return to her roots, they departed from London after five years of exile and went back to her beloved Sussex.

In keeping with her third wish, they bought a rambling, near-ruined and isolated farm called Little Doucegrove, near Brede, which Sheila had known in her childhood and which she had written about in her third novel *Spell Land*. They turned the hay loft into a chapel and then organised the building of a tiny church dedicated to St. Teresa — the "Little Flower" — in a field near the farm. Financed by her continuing success as a novelist, she and her husband filled the rôles of Sunday school teacher, verger, church cleaner and sick visitors, earning a treasured name among the Sussex farming community of all denominations for their dedication to Christian duty.

Throughout the Thirties, Sheila Kaye-Smith's name was forever before the reading public as many more books flowed from her gifted pen, almost all with a strong Sussex flavour. She turned her farm's oast house into a study, its shelves crammed with books, including many of her own, for her output was so prolific. She once described her writing as being like an iceberg . . . "by far the greater portion is out of sight". In addition to the thirteen secret novels she wrote during her last two years at school, she had 22 published books and 42 others composed in skeleton form by 1937 — all written by hand, for she spurned the use of a typewriter. Her reputation spread across the Atlantic and many of her later novels were also published in America, where she toured giving lectures to luncheon clubs in the Thirties.

But she had also received a respectable degree of recognition for the poetry and was one of those chosen by Coulson Kernahan for his critical collection of *Five More Famous Living Poets* (1928), in which he disclosed that Sheila's poems "were the expression of an inner self which she did not reveal in her novels, or even to her friends".

One of the greatest sadnesses of her life was undoubtedly the unfulfilled desire to have children, poignantly revealed in her beautiful poem *Holy Innocents*. She saw an image of the infant Christ reflected in every child born . . . and felt the world still contained its share of Herods as well as Magdalenes.

When Doctor and Mrs. Kaye-Smith went on their annual holiday — generally to the Continent — they left Sheila and her younger sister Mona with a variety of farming friends. One that she remembered fondly was Platnix

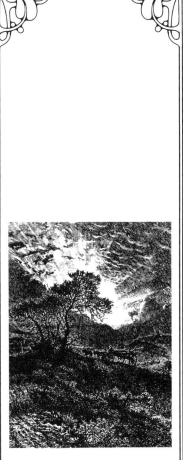

The Burning Bush

The sunrise was breaking into the mist; among the white layers of it scars appeared, spreading and dripping with light. Suddenly the expected marvel showed itself to her, not in a monstrous, frightening shape, but as a globe of fire that hung suspended in the bare, laced twigs of a thornbush on the crown of the field. She saw — she knew. It was the Burning Bush. Burning but not consumed, it stood there on the meadow slope above her, lighting the world with its radiance, so that she saw her parents' cottage, and the turnip field, and the roofs of Pickdick, and Copthorne Church, all lit as when the fire flares up mysteriously out of ashes, and lights a gloaming room.

S.K.-S. from *Susan Spray*

The Novels of Sheila Kaye-Smith

The Tramping Methodist (1908); Starbrace (1909); Spell Land (1911); Isle of Thorns; Three Against the World (1913); Sussex Gorse (1916); The Challenge to Sirius (1917); Little England (1918); Tamarisk Town (1919); Green Apple Harvest (1920); Joanna Godden (1921); The End of the House of Alard (1923); The George and the Crown (1925); Joanna Godden Married (1927); Iron and Smoke (1928); The Village Doctor (1929); Shepherds in Sackcloth (1930); The History of Susan Spray (1931); Gallybird (1932); The Ploughman's Progress; The Children's Summer (1933); Superstition Corner (1934); Selina is Older (1935); Rose Deeprose (1936); Faithful Stranger (1937); The Valiant Woman (1938); Gipsy Waggon (1939); Ember Lane (1940); Tambourine, Trumpet and Drum (1943); Summer Holiday (1947); The Lardners and the Laurelwoods (1948); Treasures of the Snow (1950); The Hidden Son (1952); Mrs. Gailey (1953); The View from the Parsonage (1954).

Other Works: John Galsworthy (1915); Mirror of the Months (1925); Anglo-Catholicism (1926); Three Ways Home (1937); Talking of Jane Austen (1944); Kitchen Fugue (1945); More Talk of Jane Austen (1950); Quartet in Heaven (1952); The Weald of Sussex and Kent (1953); All the Books of My Life (1956).

Poetry/Plays: Willow's Forge (1914); Saints in Sussex (1926); Songs, Late and Early (1931).

Mermaid Street in Rye, with the famous Mermaid Inn on the right of the picture.

Farm on the Hastings to Westfield road. She described it nostalgically in her semi-biographical novel *The Children's Summer*. Indeed many of the farms and villages mentioned in her novels can be traced by the reader today, for the names are only thinly disguised.

In his excellent book *Sheila Kaye-Smith and the Weald Country*, published just before the last war, R. Thurston Hopkins ferrets out precise locations in his search for the literary landmarks of the Sussex novelist. *Little England* is set around the villages of Dallington and Hellingly; Iden and Peasmarsh, north of Rye, are the locales of *Sussex Gorse* in which the sullen, resolute and inflexible old farmer, Reuben Backfield, still has his counterparts today.

Conster Farm, Beckley, is the siting for her book *The End of the House of Alard*; the village of Robertsbridge is the heart of *Green Apple Harvest* . . . and so it goes on.

Even the farm names have a familiar ring — Starvecrow, Dinglesden, Odiam, Blackford and Bucksteep, Little Ansdore and Worge — for Sheila Kaye-Smith steeped herself in Sussex lore and her characters and places sprang from personal knowledge.

Though not unmindful of the poverty and neglect that the commonplace country folk of East Sussex were subject to in Victorian and Edwardian times, she viewed with deep regret that fast disappearance of old-fashioned customs, speech and simple manners that followed the influx of Londoners to her beloved county. Writing an introduction to John Coker Egerton's book *Sussex Folk and Sussex Ways*, Sheila Kaye-Smith commented: "Not only are our local names being changed for us by the once-despised 'furriner', but the racy Sussex dialect, with its affinity with real English . . . and its survival of Saxon and Norman words, is crumbling away before the advancing tide of Cockney".

It was long felt by people of the south-east that only Sussex and Kent could be rightly termed "Old England" . . . everyone else was a "furriner", and all other counties were called "the sheeres", a corruption of shires. People from outside England were all called "Frenchies", regardless of their country of origin.

Sheila Kaye-Smith was unaware that death was so close when she wrote her last work *All The Books Of My Life*, for she commented in it that she would be in her seventieth year when it appeared in 1956. But she died on January 14th that year, three weeks short of her 69th birthday. Over a quarter of a century has passed since then, and despite her 50 published books, films, and many other writings, her name has quietly slipped from public memory . . . except perhaps from the minds of her loyal readers the world over, and particularly those village and farming folk who live and work in that history-steeped corner of England which will forever be known, to them at least, as "Sheila Kaye-Smith Country".

A portrait of Sheila Kaye-Smith. As a little girl she once prayed: "Please God, may I always live in the country."

The three things that have meant most to me are the country, my writing and my religion.   S.K.-S.

ALFRED NOYES

(1880-1958)

The poet and patriot who wrote in praise of England

If I ever had any doubts about the fundamental realities of religion they could always be dispelled by one memory: the light upon my father's face as he came back from early Communion. A.N.

Halfway up a steep west country hillside, a nine-year-old Victorian boy plunged into a thick wood of fir trees, scraping his knees as he wriggled through bracken and over a carpet of pine needles until he reached a tiny sunlit clearing, about 12 foot square, there to look down upon a lovely river valley. All around him were the minor miracles of Nature . . . wild flowers, birds, butterflies, and the shadows chasing across the page of the book he had carried up to his secret den. To this ecstatic spot he brought the works of Keats, Blake and Wordsworth, the novels of Dickens and Sir Walter Scott, drinking in the stirring lines that unlocked a whole treasure-house of wonder within his boyish breast.

It was in this mountain nook that the young Alfred Noyes sensed a magical undertone, a hidden meaning in the universe which led him to the life-long belief that humans were not "the guests of chance" in this world. As he later described in his book *The Unknown God* (1938), there are fragmentary glimpses of a scheme in human life, like broken bits of a great symphony which cannot be fully understood until heard in its completeness, after this our exile.

Alfred grew up to become a poet of world renown, a defender of English tradition, and a stalwart antagonist of all things ungodly. He gave us a host of immortal lines of his own — the infamous *Highwayman* who still goes riding, riding, riding through the memories of every English schoolboy in search of Bess, the landlord's black-eyed daughter; he also gave us the luring invitation to *Go down to Kew in lilac-time . . . it isn't far from London*, and thousands of us do just that in May every year. His satirical

Alfred Noyes, the great poet and patriot, photographed in his study.

verse *The Man That Was a Multitude* struck out fiercely against faddism and the trend towards obscenity in the arts, to the delight and unbridled relief of ordinary people everywhere.

Alfred Noyes sang the song of England's praises that echoed round the world, and his sense of adventure, his boyishness and his spiritual convictions remained with him to the end.

He was born on 16th September 1880, at Wolverhampton in Staffordshire, although his father — a staunch Anglican schoolteacher who had wanted to take holy orders — came from an old Wiltshire family. His mother, Amelia Adams Rowley, had a daughter and three sons of whom Alfred was the eldest. He attended Jasper House school, near his boyhood home, as one of only 37 pupils and later went up to Oxford (1898) where he excelled at rowing, being one of the crew to man the Exeter boat during Eights Week at Henley. After four years at Exeter College, on the very day of his finals, he cut the exams and went to London to see a publisher. So instead of a degree he saw his first volume of poems *The Loom of Years* produced in 1902.

Two years later, in a tiny cottage on Bagshot Heath, Surrey, he wrote *The Highwayman* within two days. The poem suggested itself to him one night when the sound of the wind in the pines gave him the first line:

The wind was a torrent of darkness among the gusty trees

It appeared shortly after that in *Blackwood's Magazine*, and was repeated in scores of anthologies and many hundreds of school books throughout England, the Empire and America, later being used as the basis for a Hollywood film.

In 1907 he married Garnet Daniels, the daughter of an American colonel who had come to England in his country's consular service, and they lived at Rottingdean in Sussex "with only £50 and my pen to support us". His wife's mother had known the two great American poets — Ralph Waldo Emerson and Henry Wadsworth Longfellow — and when Alfred and his bride visited the USA Longfellow's daughters entertained them at their home in Cambridge, Massachusetts.

In his first lecture tour of the USA, begun in 1911, his theme was peace. He later wrote: "Nearly all my writing on the subject of world peace turned upon one fact . . . that the whole future of our civilisation depends upon the co-operation of the United States and the British

Alfred in 1913 at the age of 33.

When people talk of "bounded space" I am not altogether content with the old answer of Pasteur in his address to the French Academy: "What lies beyond?" I am sceptical enough to ask, first of all, what we mean by the word "space", and whether it is anything but a relationship between one thing and another. In any case, I hold to those axioms for lack of which, as it seems to me, our modern world is ceasing to be able to think honestly and clearly. I still believe that the shortest distance between two points is a straight line. I find that not only my reason but my religion depends on the certainty that you cannot evolve plus out of minus, or Beethoven out of a cloud of hydrogen gas (the primal nebula), unless you have a very big plus working through the whole process.   A.N.

Commonwealth of Nations. Without that co-operation the world would tear itself to pieces." Yale University offered him an honorary degree of Doctor of Letters and in 1914 he took up the Murray Professorship of English Literature at Princeton University, where one of his students was the notorious Scott Fitzgerald.

In 1915 he was interviewed by a young man from the *New York Times* — the budding poet Joyce Kilmer, who had just had his own poem *Trees* published. Noyes recognised the beauty of the lyric:

> *Poems are made by fools like me*
> *But only God can make a tree*

and felt that there was something very strong and well balanced in Kilmer himself, who died a mere two years later, aged 31. Another friend of his Princeton days was Sir Cecil Spring-Rice, the British Ambassador to Washington, and writer of that most stirring English verse *I Vow To Thee My Country*.

Alfred returned to England early in 1916 and because of his knowledge of American affairs was invited to join the News Department of the Foreign Office, the nucleus of what was to become the Ministry of Information, and he made occasional visits to the Front. After the war, while a literary critic for the *Daily Graphic*, he entered into a long series of controversial correspondence with Thomas Hardy, for the two were on opposite sides of the fence in life's great debate. Hardy, as his Wessex novels show, was a pessimist and an agnostic. Noyes on the other hand was an optimist, believing firmly in God as the Creator of all things. During the early Twenties he spent several months of each year in a flat overlooking Cadogan Gardens, and the daily sight of people from all walks of life entering the RC church of St. Mary's opposite his apartment was to have an increasing influence on his previously total Anglican outlook.

In 1926, while on holiday at St. Jean de Luz in southern France, Alfred and his wife visited a chapel in the Pyrenees and together spoke about their possible conversion to Catholicism. A week later Garnet died, and within a year of her death Alfred himself was received into the Catholic Church, as his literary contemporary and friend G.K. Chesterton had been four years earlier.

In the autumn of 1927 he married Mary Weld-Blundell, widow of Richard Weld-Blundell of Lulworth Castle, Dorset, a lieutenant in the Coldstream Guards who was

Mary Weld-Blundell, who became Alfred's bride in 1927.

It was like recovering one's memory after a long period of aphasia; and it was also the recovery of the road that not only ran back through history, but went forward to the ultimate end for which man was made. There was a sense in which it rejuvenated the whole world, and brought to life a thousand characters that had hitherto been only faded figures in a historical tapestry.

It was a renaissance of the mind, in which the literature and philosophy of all the ages acquired a new and vital beauty.

A.N. (Upon becoming a Catholic)

A SONG OF ENGLAND

by ALFRED NOYES

Photograph: *One of the "leafy lanes of England" . . . at the village of Bossington in Somerset.*

There is a song of England that none shall ever sing;
So sweet it is and fleet it is
That none whose words are now as fleet as birds upon the wing,
And regal as her mountains
And radiant as the fountains
Of rainbow-coloured sea-spray that every wave can fling
Against the cliffs of England, the sturdy cliffs of England,
Could more than seem to dream of it,
Or catch one flying gleam of it,
Above the seas of England that never cease to sing.

There is a song of England that only lovers know;
So rare it is and fair it is,
Oh, like a fairy rose it is upon a drift of snow.
So cold and sweet and sunny,
So full of hidden honey,
So like a flight of butterflies where rose and lily blow
Along the lanes of England, the leafy lanes of England;
When flowers are at their vespers
And full of little whispers,
The boys and girls of England shall sing it as they go.

There is a song of England that haunts her hours of rest;
The calm of it and balm of it
Are breathed from every hedgerow that blushes to the West;
From cottage doors that nightly
Cast their welcome out so brightly
On the lanes where laughing children are lifted and caressed
By the tenderest hands in England, hard and blistered hands of England;
And from the restful sighing
Of the sleepers that are lying
With the arms of God around them on the night's contented breast.

There is a song of England that wanders in the wind;
So sad it is and glad it is
That men who hear it madden and their eyes are wet and blind,
For the lowlands and the highlands
Of the unforgotten islands,
For the Islands of the Blessed, and the rest they cannot find
As they grope in dreams to England and the love they left in England;
Little feet that danced to meet them,
And the lips that used to greet them,
And the watcher at the window in the home they left behind.

There is a song of England that thrills the beating blood
With burning cries and yearning
Tides of hidden aspiration hardly known or understood;
Aspirations of the creature
Tow'rds the unity of Nature;
Sudden chivalries revealing whence the longing is renewed
In the men that live for England, live and love and die for England;
By the light of their desire
They shall blindly blunder higher
To a wider, grander Kingdom and a deeper, nobler Good.

There is a song of England that only God can hear;
So gloriously victorious,
It soars above the choral stars that sing the Golden Year;
Till even the cloudy shadows
That wander o'er her meadows
In silent purple harmonies declare His glory there,
Above the hills of England, the billowy hills of England,
While heaven rolls and ranges
Through all the myriad changes
That mirror God in music to the mortal eye and ear.

The Last of the Books

Is it too strange to think
That, when all life at last from earth
    is gone,
And round the sun's pale blink
Our desolate planet wheels its ice
    and stone,
Housed among storm-proof walls
    there yet may abide
Defying long the venoms of decay,
A still dark throng of books, dumb
    books of song
And tenderest fancies born of youth
    and May.

A quiet remembering host,
Out-living the poor dust that gave
    them birth,
Unvisited by even a wandering ghost,
But treasuring still the music of our
    earth,
In little fading hieroglyphs they shall
    bear
Through death and night, the legend
    of our Spring,
And how the lilac scented the bright
    air
When hearts throbbed warm, and
    lips could kiss and sing.

And, ere that record fail,
Strange voyagers from a mightier
    planet come
On wingèd ships that through the
    void can sail
And gently alight upon our ancient
    home;
Strange voices echo, and strange
    flares explore,
Strange hands, with curious weapons,
    burst these bars,
Lift the brown volumes to the light
    once more,
And bear their stranger secrets
    through the stars.

                     A.N.

Lisle Combe, the writer's magnificent house on the Isle of Wight.

killed in the First World War. In time they had three children — Hugh, Veronica and Margaret — and lived in London's Hanover Terrace overlooking Regent's Park.

The late Twenties were a time of violent social and moral change, and Alfred the traditionalist was at the forefront of those who campaigned against the most flagrant of these excesses. Notably, he attacked the publication of *Ulysses* by James Joyce, one of the first of the so-called liberal books, and defended traditional poetry against the modernist cult of Edith Sitwell. Noyes enjoyed experimenting with rhyme and metre, whereas the modernists dispensed with it, and he once remarked in answer to those who dubbed him an old-fashioned romantic: "I am quite content to be behind the times when I see the ghastly people who are abreast of it".

In 1929 he visited the Isle of Wight and purchased Lisle Combe, a small estate on the southern cliffs with reputedly the loveliest garden on the island. It is still owned and occupied by members of the Noyes family and its gardens are opened to the public on Easter Sunday. Alfred wrote about Lisle Combe in his book *Orchard's Bay* (1939) . . . the long house of warm grey stone, with twisted red Elizabethan chimneys. It was here that his second idyllic marriage flourished, among the flowers and ferns of an old garden "where the beeches spread in benediction over its lovers".

Lisle Combe was Alfred's Avalon, the place where he desired to live and hoped to die — a wish that came true. From the book-lined study overlooking the smooth lawns

122

A remarkable photograph of the day in 1933 when Queen Mary called for tea and walked with the poet in the gardens of his home.

he wrote: "If, as many wise men have thought, the next world is only the other and the more beautiful aspect of the tapestry we are weaving here, I would ask nothing better on the other side of death".

The Noyes family sold their London home to H.G. Wells and settled to a life of mellow, domestic happiness on the Isle. Their many friends and visitors reads like a Who's Who of the times — Chesterton, Dean Inge, Hilaire Belloc, H. de Vere Stacpoole, J.B. Priestley, Emperor Haile Selassie and Admiral Jellicoe. In 1933 Queen Mary came ashore from the Royal Yacht *Victoria and Albert*, anchored off Cowes, visiting the Noyes family for tea and wandering in the gardens with Alfred, whose work she knew well. She repeated the visit the following year.

When it first became fashionable among the artistic fringes of London society to applaud the obscene, and to hail profanity as a new form of literary beauty, Alfred Noyes stood up and objected. He lent his name and the power of his pen to those voices raised in protest, on both

At our interview he (Mussolini) strutted and tossed his head about in a manner that would have been ludicrous if it had not been for the glare of his eyes, which continually showed their white rings. They were the eyes not of a man but of a wild creature, and human communication seemed no more possible with them than with those of a tiger. However, when I thought about it later, I was not sure whether their strange glare expressed ferocity or a secret and intense fear of the terrible forces that held him in their grip. One could almost think now that those white-ringed eyes had some uncanny prescience of his own ghastly end.   A.N.

Go Down to Kew in Lilac-Time

by ALFRED NOYES

There's a barrel-organ carolling across a golden street
In the City as the sun sinks low;
And the music's not immortal; but the world has made it sweet
And fulfilled it with the sunset glow;
And it pulses through the pleasures of the City and the pain
That surround the singing organ like a large eternal light;
And they've given it a glory and a part to play again
In the Symphony that rules the day and night.

Go down to Kew in lilac-time, in lilac-time, in lilac-time;
Go down to Kew in lilac-time (it isn't far from London!)
And you shall wander hand in hand with love in summer's wonderland;
Go down to Kew in lilac-time (it isn't far from London!)

The cherry-trees are seas of bloom and soft perfume and sweet perfume,
The cherry-trees are seas of bloom (and oh, so near to London!)
And there they say, when dawn is high and all the world's a blaze of sky
The cuckoo, though he's very shy, will sing a song for London.

Daffodil-time at Kew beside the Temple of Aeolus.

The nightingale is rather rare and yet they say you'll hear him there
At Kew, at Kew in lilac-time (and oh, so near to London!)
The linnet and the throstle, too, and after dark the long halloo
And golden-eyed *tu-whit, tu-whoo* of owls that ogle London.

For Noah hardly knew a bird of any kind that isn't heard
At Kew, at Kew in lilac-time (and oh, so near to London!)
And when the rose begins to pout and all the chestnut spires are out
You'll hear the rest without a doubt, all chorussing for London: —

Come down to Kew in lilac-time, in lilac-time, in lilac-time;
Come down to Kew in lilac-time (it isn't far from London!)
And you shall wander hand in hand with love in summer's wonderland;
Come down to Kew in lilac-time (it isn't far from London!)

It is the function of all great art, in fact, to establish a right relationship between things temporal and things eternal. So that what may appear chaotic and fragmentary in our daily life, seen in another aspect is part of a perfect whole. The harmonies of great art are symbolical, a little cosmos, enabling us to apprehend a greater cosmos that transcends our faculties.

A.N.

Perhaps the most beautiful line in Shakespeare is the cry of Hamlet, "Absent thee from felicity awhile", but it fades into insignificance before the words upon which Christendom was founded. These last have one quality which differentiates them from all other human words. Merely human words, even those of the greatest poets, may express the desire of the moth for the star, the desire of the exile for a better country, but the words upon which Christendom was founded come to us from the centre: "I am the Resurrection and the Life".

A.N.

The boys of Brockley Central School in London were an eager audience when Alfred Noyes gave them a talk about poetry.

sides of the Atlantic. His brilliant verse, skilled oratory and incisive correspondence held aloft the banners of decency, and gave ordinary people a clearer view of life's worthwhile goals.

It has always puzzled many that the Poet Laureateship was never offered to him who had given so much to his country. Nor was his name picked by political promoters for inclusion in the Honours List, except for a modest CBE. In the quest for honesty and truth, no doubt, many corns are trod upon. And Alfred Noyes was an outspoken and fearless crusader, regardless of self. But his work is his testimony, and as such will outlast all the baubles that officialdom can bestow.

As the Second World War approached he wrote of the political thrombosis of the times: "I feel that in the past 20 years or so many of the English have been asleep — and their nightmares are now in charge of our destiny". In 1940 he undertook an exhausting lecture tour of America and Canada, involving much long-distance travel often including two separate engagements daily, many miles apart, to several thousand people. His theme, apart from English literature, was that the spread of Communism was one of the most dangerous ingredients in the world. But the mounting tension his talks caused in him gave rise to the dreaded corneal disease glaucoma and gradually his eyesight began to fail. Within two years he was unable to read, and when

126

Alfred Noyes had many of the leading figures of his day visit him at Lisle Combe, among them Dean Inge.

Whatever the defects and limitations of my own work may be, I have truly lived the art of poetry and given the best of my life to it.   A.N.

he returned to England in 1949 he underwent further eye surgery . . . but the world gradually closed in around him and he spent the remaining years of his life at Lisle Combe, where he knew every inch of the ground, cloaked in misty darkness. Almost daily, despite his virtual blindness, he swam in the cold waters of the English Channel which lap the shingled shore of Orchard's Bay, fronting his house, being guided back to the beach by the voice of his loving wife. He died there, after a short illness, in June 1958 at the age of 77.

There are many who can recall the pride and pageantry of pre-war Empire Day celebrations in England, and not a few perhaps who were present in Hyde Park for the 1931 event when, before a crowd of 50,000 people from all over the country, Dame Madge Kendall read the stirring poem *The Exiles* specially written by Alfred Noyes for Empire Day, which was broadcast throughout the English speaking world.

By such words he became a confirmed patriot in the English public's heart. But to all who knew him, Alfred Noyes was not just a poet of splendid vigour and lyrical beauty. He was also a Christian of high calibre. And perhaps most of all, a true English gentleman.

The Main Works of Alfred Noyes

The Loom of Years (1902); The Flower of Old Japan (1903); Poems (1904); Drake (1906-8); Forty Singing Seamen (1907); Collected Poems (1910); The Torch-Bearers (1922-30); The Unknown God (1934); Voltaire (1936); Orchard's Bay (1939); Collected Poems (1950); Two Worlds For Memory (autobiography, 1953); Letter To Lucien (1956).

FLORA KLICKMANN

(1867-1958)

The Queen of Flower Patch Country

To young people, I would say this. Don't let yourself be led astray by every new doctrine which is proclaimed, no matter how convincing the speaker may be, and no matter how many other people may be taking up the idea with fervour. Use your common sense. Have nothing to do with any theories or schemes or plans for reconstruction that are in any way contrary to God's teaching in the Bible. F.K.

There twice a day the Severn fills;
The salt sea-water passes by,
And hushes half the babbling Wye,
And makes a silence in the hills.

ALFRED, LORD TENNYSON (*In Memoriam*)

Eighty years ago, the Great Western Railway's chocolate and stone-coloured main line express from Paddington to South Wales thundered into the smoke-blackened station at Chepstow, and out stepped a smart London lady wearing an enormous, though fashionable, hat. She crossed over the platforms to board the branch line puffer that thrice daily wound its way along the single track skirting the banks of the meandering River Wye which marks the border between England and Monmouthshire.

With a snort and a rumble the little train chugged through lush orchards, placid meadows, past simple cottages with a few scratching hens about and a clothes-line of pinafores and collarless shirts; then screeched its way ever upwards into the rocky hills and along tree-lined ledges that look down upon the twisting, tumbling river below. Finally, with a shrill toot and a shriek of brakes, the train stopped at the village of Tintern, and the London lady alighted onto the narrow platform to be met by eager porters and a resplendent station-master who tipped his cap politely — for this was at a time when the railwaymen of England had elevated courtesy from being a mere duty to that of a fine art.

Old Bob, owner of a smart waggonette pulled by a pair of prancing mares, jingled his way forward and safely

*Flora Klickmann with Dandy, the little dog mentioned in
many of her Flower Patch books.*

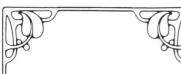

The Flower Patch

I took a cottage in the country on a day when I had got to the fag-end of the very last straw, and felt I could not endure for another minute the screech of the trains, the honking of motors, the clanging of bells, the clatter of milk-carts, the grind-and-screel of electric cars, the ever-ringing telephone, the rattle and roar of the general traffic, the all-pervading odour of petrol, and the many other horrors that make both day and night hideous in our great city, and reduce the workers to nervous wreckage.

The cottage has been so arranged that not one solitary thing within its walls shall bear any relation to the city left far behind, and nothing is allowed to remind the occupants of the business rush, the social scramble, and the electric-light-type of existence that have become integral parts of modern life in towns.

Here, to keep my idle hands from mischief, I made me a Flower-patch . . .

This is the spot where, for me, a new life begins; where unconsciously I draw my breath with a deep intake, and suddenly feel the past slipping from me; the noise and din, the sordidness and care of the city fade into the background and become nothing more substantial than some remote nightmare.

Here in this Valley of Peace and Quietness my dreams become realities. And best of all, here God seems to lay His Hand on tired heart and tired brain; and I find myself saying "This is the rest wherewith ye may cause the weary to rest, and this is the refreshing".

F.K. from *The Flower Patch Among the Hills*

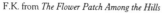

Flora's cottage at Brockweir as it looked 10 years ago. When she lived in the house she refused to have electricity connected, preferring oil lamps.

gathered the lady and her accoutrements into the bosom of his carriage for the last part of her journey, a mile drive along narrow lanes lined with woodbine and primrose, to a little white gate leading to a cottage set in a garden of riotous beauty.

This blessed spot was to become the mystical heart of Flower Patch country . . . the homespun world of gentility and peace loved by millions and created by the elegant lady of our narrative — Flora Klickmann, then Editor of the famous *Girl's Own Paper* and soon to be the author of a string of best-selling "Flower Patch" novels.

Through her words of commonsense philosophy Flora influenced the thinking of countless thousands of young women from 1908, when she first became the paper's Editor, until the Thirties. Questions of fashion, matrimony, social behaviour, domestic achievement, careers, and the hinted-at personal problems that formed the embryo of today's "agony columns" in the women's weeklies, were all influenced by Flora Klickmann. And she gained much of her inspiration and succour from the literary wonderland she created around her Flower Patch in the western borderland of England.

Flora had known the Wye Valley from early childhood when she had visited relatives on her mother's side for holidays. But she was brought up in London, having been born there — at Bloomsbury — on 26th January, 1867, the second of six children. Three of them died at various stages of childhood and Flora's mother was so shocked and distressed that her husband, a German immigrant, moved to the country-like atmosphere of the south bank of the Thames on medical advice. At that time Flora herself was also ill with quinsy, a severe inflammation of the throat, and while she was in bed she was given a pretty doll's tea set. This began in her a lifelong interest in dolls' houses and furniture, which she rightly regarded as an art form.

The move to a new family home at Millbrook Road, Brixton, brought Flora into contact with music and literary circles, centred on the Crystal Palace, which in time led her into journalism and to writing her Flower Patch stories. Her mother's love of Nature, and flowers in particular, also had a lasting effect on Flora's life for she in turn became an expert in gardening matters and was able to name and discuss all of the many hundreds of wild flowers that abounded around her Wye Valley cottage.

Flora had every intention of becoming a concert musician, studying at the Trinity College of Music and later at the Royal College of Organists. She was a frequent visitor to the Crystal Palace in the great days of the Saturday Concerts where Britain's first permanent orchestra was established and where great musicians and composers came to perform. Flora was recruited to "turn the pages" for some of the famous pianists and after much concentrated study she was invited to play the great American organ in a concert — the youngest woman ever to do so, for she was still in pigtails.

But the nervous strain of over-work eventually caused her to collapse and she was ordered to take a complete rest. Her doctor declared she must forsake all hope of a concert career for her illness had left her with a life-long heart weakness. In one moment of depression, while alone in her room, she looked in the mirror and said: "You are twenty-one and your life is finished".

But she underestimated her own hidden strength and talent, for after taking up a post as piano tutor at the Chapel Royal she began writing articles for the various journals, primarily on music. Then she became assistant editor on a woman's magazine of the day, *Sylvia's Home Journal*, and eventually helped to launch *The Windsor Magazine*, a highly popular periodical at the turn of the century which included the works of many leading literary names of the day such as Rudyard Kipling, Eden Philpotts, Edith Nesbit, and the brilliant caricaturist Phil May. Yet the Wye

Flora in 1912 wearing one of her magnificent hats and (below) the cover of Sylvia's Home Journal, *the woman's magazine on which she was assistant editor.*

131

When I am badly in the depths, I know of no surer way to restore my mind than a long walk across the hills. Some people need human companionship, but personally, I can do very well by myself under such circumstances (always provided that I don't meet a cow likewise on a walking tour).

F.K. from *The Flower Patch Among the Hills* (1916)

An example of the beautiful artwork which adorned The Girl's Own Paper. *Flora Klickmann became its editor in 1908.*

Valley was never far from her thoughts and her first book, *The Ambitions of Jenny Ingram*, published in 1902, was the story of a young woman who left her home in the Wye Valley to take up a career in London journalism.

Flora herself quickly built up a fine reputation as a lively and versatile journalist, occasionally being responsible for the entire editing of *The Windsor Magazine*. She later joined the Literary Department of the Bible Society and transformed the "stiff and starchy" bulletin of the Wesleyan Methodist Missionary Society into a new-look magazine (retitled *The Foreign Field*) which built up the largest sale of any missionary periodical then published in Britain.

She was then invited to become Editor of *The Girl's Own Paper* following the death of its founder-editor, bachelor Charles Peters. Published by the Religious Tract Society, which also owned *The Boy's Own Paper*, it quickly raced ahead of its male counterpart and reached a massive, world-wide circulation. It was looked upon as a social "bible" by the thousands of young ladies throughout the country who devoured its stories and advice. From such a position it set fashion trends and could dictate on all manner of domestic questions. Flora's position, therefore, was vested with the sort of power that some politicians only ever dream about. But she exercised it with a great sense of responsibility and forethought . . . often to the detriment of her own health.

She became a literary lioness in an almost exclusively male world, for Fleet Street was as exacting a theatre of rivalry then as it has been ever since. But the pace soon began to tell as Flora strove to lift the magazine to even greater heights. She brought in new ideas, new writers and

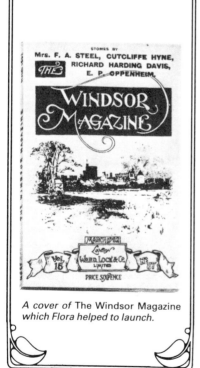

A cover of The Windsor Magazine *which Flora helped to launch.*

132

Flower Patch Country today, with the village of Brockweir on the banks of the River Wye.

artists, and introduced the new colour printing techniques to make the G.O.P. one of the most beautiful journals ever produced. Under her direction the magazine prospered and Flora began receiving a mountain of mail from readers in every country of the English-speaking world.

To ease the stress and strain of her London life, Flora travelled west to Brockweir whenever possible. She had earlier persuaded one of her mother's relatives to sell her the tiny cottage in the hills she had known as a child, and it was to there she repaired on a Friday afternoon for a weekend of rest and relaxation among the wild flowers and friendly folk of the Valley, dominated by the beautiful ruin of Tintern Abbey.

Brockweir in those days still retained a fairyland air about it. On Flora's childhood visits the village was isolated from the main Chepstow to Monmouth road and the railway station at Tintern a few hundred yards away, by the gushing river which had to be crossed by flat-bottomed ferry. But in 1906 a latticed iron bridge was built, opening it up to visitors and easing the arrival of railway passengers like Flora.

Once inside her cottage, with her dog Dandy and housemaid Abigail, Flora would forget all about her exciting life in London and wind down, among the bluebells and the simple, homely folk of the Valley. She once wrote: "I have laid my battered brain on pillows in some of the largest

People . . .

We know the girl who laughs at what our grandmothers called 'modesty' and assures us that reticence in manners or conversation is quite out of place, impossible, in fact, if a girl wants to 'get on'. We also come across those who make money the criterion of worth, people who measure everything by the cash standard and who consider that a big income condones every sort of moral failing. Add to these, the people who look upon work as an evil or at best a misfortune, those who deny all obligation to serve others, those who pour contempt on parental and every other type of authority, those who consider the restless pursuit of excitement the acme of living and the quiet performance of one's duties as the quintessence of dullness . . . in fact, add all those who are indifferent to the laws of God as set forth in the Bible and you get a general idea of a certain class of people who are preventing the world regaining spiritual health and keeping it in a state of chaos.

F.K. from *The Shining Way*, 1923

133

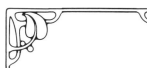

Buttercups have not yet come into their own as garden subjects. But they will, one of these days! My own little experiments with these flowers make me sure they will be treasured in gardens some day, when our fields are built over. They are capable of doing so much more than one usually imagines.

F.K. from *The Flower Patch Garden Book*

This is not a book for the great among flower growers. Nor is it for the highly experienced. Nor for the owners of gardens who specialise in under-gardeners. It is merely some random memos, made by one who doesn't know much, but who manages to keep moderately sane in the midst of that grinding machine called London, by thinking at the day's end of the high hills which though far away, are ever near to those who have once looked upon them, and loved their flowers, and ferns and trees and singing waters.

F.K. from *The Flower Patch Garden Book*

The Post Office and General Store in Brockweir. From here large sackfuls of mail from all over the world were taken to Flora's cottage.

hotels in the world; but I have never known in any of them the peaceful rest that is to be found in my cottage bedroom, despite its sloping roof".

The Flower Patch stories came into being by an odd circumstance. Flora was, in her own words, "viciously prodding up bindweed out of the cottage garden with a steel kitchen poker" when a telegraph boy opened the gate bringing a message from her London office to say that there was a hitch in regard to the copyright of an article due to appear in the magazine's next issue, and could she wire back what was to replace it since the printing machines were then at a standstill!

Under ordinary circumstances she would have instantly substituted a feature held on file — had she been in London. "But such is the witchery of the Flower Patch", she wrote in one of her books, "that no sooner do I get inside the gate than I forget every mortal thing connected with my office . . . and because I could think of nothing else on the spur of the moment I threw down the poker and went indoors and wrote about the cottage and the hills".

When her article on the Flower Patch was published in the magazine readers from all over the world wrote by the bagful begging for a continuation . . . and so the legend began, and continued for over 30 years. Even now her many volumes are chanced upon by book browsers and some literary pilgrims come to the Wye Valley to wander around Brockweir and Tintern seeking to pick up the traces of Flower Patch happenings, and to follow in the footsteps of Flora Klickmann. But it isn't easy, for such is the relentless march of time that Nature has enveloped much of the floral wonderland beneath a thick canopy of briar and wild fern, and only a few old folk in Brockweir still recall the reclusive old lady who lived in the house on the hill.

Flora's London home was at Sydenham and it was there, in 1912, that she collapsed from overwork. After her recovery she married one of the executives of her publishing company, Mr. Ebenezer Henderson Smith, in 1913. As a wedding gift he bought her a fine Victorian house called "Sylvan View" in the hills above Brockweir, and in time this also became "the Flower Patch" as Flora's cottage had been known. Flora considered the house's name "too suburban" so she called it "Buttercup Cottage" in her books.

One of Flora's cousins, Phyllis Warne, of Middlesbrough, often visited the house between the wars and recalls:

"When Flora was at home, there was always a small, embroidered cloth spread at one end of the long dining table with little vases or bowls with arrangements of wild flowers in them. Flora really had a 'thing' about wild flowers, and I remember how blazing she was once when a man had been found on her land digging up primroses and ferns by the roots to sell in the markets. Nothing could make her angrier than trespassers, even if they were admiring readers who would find out where she lived, wander up through the woods below her house, dodging the path and the gates, and suddenly appearing through the bushes across the lawns near her house.

"When invited friends or members of the family visited her, however, it was delightful to walk with her and Dandy, the dog, through her favourite sequence of winding paths, by woods and meadows, and the large informal garden, whilst she pointed out and named every flower, both wild and garden. Her marvellous doll's house stood in a large corner cupboard in the drawing room. I used to be fascinated by it, and gaze into it by the hour. It was complete in every well proportioned detail — it was a collector's piece, as was her work box."

Visitors to the Flower Patch were often surprised by the lack of mains electricity. Flora set her face against such modern innovations at her country home. She was

Theories

At the present moment, we are suffering from a deluge of useless theories and suggestions and recipes for re-organising the world in general and our own nation in particular. Some of these are merely freakish; others are either insane or dangerously unhealthy, but they are invariably labelled 'new' ideas, and those who put them forward assure us that here is the one great answer for the ills of our time. However, many of the so-called new ideas that are being pressed upon weary humanity at the moment are anything but new. They are older than civilisation and were flourishing gaily when man was a primitive savage. We don't need them introduced at this stage of this world's career.

In most cases, there is a disposition to kick down all the good work of the past, to belittle the achievements of other generations, to regard as worthless the painstaking efforts of the men and women who laid the foundations of our civilisation or added beauty to its structure. These dangerous theories usually include a whole-hearted contempt of the virtues — 'the old fashioned virtues' as we call them now — just as if virtue went in and out of current use like ear-rings or large sleeves.

F.K.

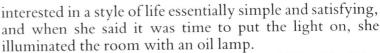

Flora Klickmann's name prominently displayed on the cover of The Girl's Own Paper and Woman's Magazine in 1921. It ceased publication soon after her death in 1958.

I can never understand the present-day craze for banishing every daisy from the domestic lawn.

Where can you see a more lovely and enheartening sight than the velvety turf of an English lawn starred all over with little daisies, their golden eyes gazing up at the sun; or, at sunset, going to sleep with pink-tipped little frills to protect their tiny heads?

The real truth is, daisies — like sunshine and water — are so plentiful that we have ceased to value them, and entirely forget to be grateful for them. But, picture to yourself, if you can, what our land would be like without them.

F.K. from *The Flower Patch Garden Book*

interested in a style of life essentially simple and satisfying, and when she said it was time to put the light on, she illuminated the room with an oil lamp.

Flora became a great expert on the natural life of the Wye Valley and was a pioneer ecologist, representing a life style based on a kinship with Creation that is much advanced today. The appeal of London waned and she spent more and more of her time at Brockweir, until *The Girl's Own Paper* was virtually edited from the Flower Patch. Flora's first main book *The Flower Patch Among the Hills* (1916) was a bestseller, as was its follow-up *Between the Larch Woods and the Weir* (1917). Although many other books were to follow — the last, *Weeding the Flower Patch*, appeared in 1948 when she was 81! — these first two titles have a special charm. They both capture a way of life, observations on local characters and events, and the beauty of Nature that together make a great tribute to the Wye Valley. She describes, for example, the delights of travelling on the single line railway from Chepstow to Brockweir; the characters that came to her bird table, blue tits, robins, jays, wood pigeons and the rest; local temperance meetings and quaint characters threat; bonfires; snowdrifts; flowers, ferns and other rural wonders.

Flora continued writing and editing through the 1920s, producing several new books. One of these has a special relevance to our troubled times: *Mending Your Nerves* (1924) was a book of commonsense advice and insights into anxiety. In 1931, the year following her husband's retirement, Flora went to live permanently at her Flower Patch and gave up the Editorship of *The Girl's Own Paper*. It certainly marked the end of a great era in women's journalism. Through the pages of that magazine, Flora championed many causes, including women's status in the professions; protection of the countryside; consumer education and housecraft, and always literature and the arts. Much and perhaps most of this material was written by hand (Flora never used a typewriter) at Brockweir. Also in 1931, *The Lady with the Crumbs* was published, with illustrations by H.M. Brock. This was a children's book, but the Flower Patch featured in the plot.

During the 1930s, three more major works were published: *Visitors to the Flower Patch; Delicate Fuss*, a novel; and *The Flower Patch Garden Book*, the last of these being a useful book on garden management, full of good sense for our own times, for Flora today would have used

Flora at work in her study.

"Nature's way" rather than factory-made chemical products in her garden.

By the time this last book was reprinted in 1937, Flora had celebrated her seventieth birthday. It was in that year that her husband died, in his late eighties. Flora, by now something of a recluse, received very many letters of sympathy. She lived until November 1958, an old lady dwelling on her memories and surrounded by the many beautiful objects she had collected over the years. Apart from one or two legacies to friends, this remarkable collection was sold, as she had requested, in aid of worthwhile missionary causes. Flora was laid to rest in the lawn surrounding "the little white Moravian church" in the centre of Brockweir where her husband used to preach occasionally.

Flora's nephew, the Reverend Brian Kingslake (his father changed the family name from Klickmann to Kingslake during the First World War, owing to the anti-German feeling present in England at that time) retains fond memories of his aunt and his visits to the Flower Patch.

"When I was twelve, I had rheumatic fever. This was a painful experience, but it proved to be well worth while because, as a result of it, the incredible happened! I was invited to accompany Aunt Flora and Uncle Henderson on a three months' visit to the Flower Patch, to convalesce. It is quite beyond my powers to describe the impact made

One of Flora Klickmann's cookery books which she described as "compact in size, and printed in a clear direct manner, with the information put in so straightforward and simple a style that the most inexperienced can use it with a certainty of success".

If you are not quite sure, in your secret heart, whether your wish to take up some special work in which you are interested is due solely to your desire to devote your life to God's service — or whether a little of your personal preference has crept in, ask yourself if you would be willing to give up all idea of this special work and instead go and look after some invalid relative who may be none too easy to live with, and none too grateful for what you do.

If God were to tell you today that He is not wanting someone at this moment to sing for Him, or to go out as a missionary, but He is wanting someone to witness for Him by living a bright shining life at home (where it may be there are some not entirely in sympathy with your ideals) would you find it just as easy to say: "Here am I, Lord, send me"?

F.K. from *The Path to Fame*

A lovely portrait of Flora in later life.

The magnificent ruin of Tintern Abbey.

upon me by this first visit to the Wye Valley. The grand and spacious manner of living at "Flower Patch House", together with the enchanting beauties of the countryside, quite overwhelmed me.

"Aunt Flora, for all her charm, was an autocratic personality and you had to do exactly what she said, without question. But, if you were prepared to yield up your free will you had a wonderful time. And oh! what joy when she released me to go out alone for an hour, over the hills and far away, to scramble through dense woods full of bluebells and wood anemones, or stand reverently in "the cathedral of the larches", or clamber up waterfalls to emerge at the top with a breath-taking view of the River Wye serpenting away to the Bristol Channel, with Tintern Abbey slumbering at my feet.

"The main room of the house was her study, where she sat tall and upright at a big desk, with a bulging wastepaper basket at her feet. Sketches and paintings were pinned up all over the walls. She had no typewriter, but answered her vast correspondence with a gold-nibbed pen which she dipped in a monumental inkwell. She said that she needed the dipping motion to get inspiration. If anyone presented her with a fountain pen, she used it for squirting water into small plant pots! A secretary came down from London to help her sometimes, but, for the most part, Flora controlled her great magazine by mail — as the local postwoman knew to her cost, toiling up the hill every morning with a big sack full of letters and packages.

"I was sometimes called to the study and given a *National Geographic Magazine* to read, and I had to tell her afterwards what the articles were about. Or I had to write a review of a new adventure book — a valuable exercise for budding authors. She told me stories from the turbulent history of the English-Welsh border country, and took me to Chepstow and Raglan Castles which she made alive for me. I was officially appointed "Chief Forest Ranger of Offa's Dyke", the old boundary line which ran through her woods. I had to learn the songs of the birds, and she taught me how to rear a bald chick which had fallen from its nest, by pushing wet, rolled oats into its gaping beak. Trees, flowers, grasses, mosses — I had not known that there was so much Nature lore to be acquired.

"I was in Africa when we had news of her death. I learned also that I had inherited a cottage on the estate, and the pull back to England was strong. But what would the Flower Patch be like, without its presiding genius? Aunt Flora is now regaining her youth in the spiritual world, and tending the flower gardens of Heaven."

Today her many books are out of print, and *The Girl's Own Paper* is remembered by only a few, for it ceased publication soon after Flora's death.

A visitor seeking to find Flower Patch country today would need a car, for the branch line to Tintern and Brockweir was closed thirty years ago. But the station-house, signal box and sidings have been turned into a delightful picnic spot as part of a Wye Valley nature trail, and the little white church of Moravian origin still gleams on the Gloucestershire side of the river, holding in the heart of its well-kept churchyard a small marble tablet to the memory of the woman who wrote so feelingly of the part of England she loved best of all.

In any case, the pilgrim need only walk in the hills above Brockweir in the summertime, when the tiny lanes are heady with rosemary and hedge parsley, to sense at once the spirit that so inspired Flora Klickmann into creating her literary wonderland . . . of Flower Patch country.

THE WORKS OF FLORA KLICKMANN

Flower Patch stories:

The Flower Patch Among the Hills (1916); Between the Larch Woods and the Weir (1917); Trail of the Ragged Robin (1921); Flower Patch Neighbours (1928); Visitors to the Flower Patch (1931); The Flower Patch Garden Book (1933); Weeding the Flower Patch (1948).

Other novels:

The Ambitions of Jenny Ingram (1902); Delicate Fuss (1932); Carillon of Scarpa (1925).

Children's books:

The Lady with the Crumbs (1931); Mystery of the Windflower Wood (1932).

General works:

Lure of the Pen (1919); The Shining Way (1923); Mending Your Nerves (1924); The Path to Fame (1925); Little Book of Helpful Verse (1925); Many Questions (1928).

The Moravian church in Brockweir where Flora and her husband are buried.

Arthur Mee, the great Editor, writer and crusader of Fleet Street.

ARTHUR MEE

(1875-1943)

The Christian Crusader of Fleet Street

Around the time of Queen Victoria's golden jubilee, and long before the hysteria of films and football had come to smother the minds of the populace with irrelevant diversions, the local newspapers of England stimulated the inquiring minds of the day with long and detailed reports on all and every topic. Parliament, and proceedings, political speeches, law reports, police cases, public acts and private follies, all found expression in the tightly-packed columns of the nation's ever-vigilant Press. Most large towns had more than one daily or evening newspaper published locally, while even the remotest village boasted its own weekly, with the result that England had a strong seam of its working population fully abreast of current affairs.

In many households, father would spend an hour or more every evening after supper catching up on local and national happenings. Sometimes a bright child would be chosen to read the reports out loud, so enabling father and mother to perform other tasks while still keeping abreast of the news.

It was for precisely this function that Henry Mellors, the local baker at Stapleford in Nottinghamshire, secured the services of a bright and eager schoolboy . . . twelve-year-old Arthur Henry Mee, eldest boy in a family of ten who lived in the lace-making township. Every night young Arthur, a sober-sided lad for his age, would attend Mellors Bakery and read aloud the Parliamentary reports of the previous day while the old baker kneaded his dough and fired his ovens.

Doubtless the only immediate reward for Arthur was

It will save us from infinite sorrow to love books. It will keep us calm in a thousand storms to have as our companions the great spirits of all time. We are building up, when we love books and read them, a bank of delights on which we can draw a cheque of happiness whenever we please, and no millionaire can buy such happiness with his gold.

A.M. from *Wonderful Year*, 1943

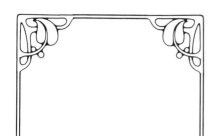

1940

(Extracts from the book of that year,
by Arthur Mee)

Nineteen-forty will probably be remembered in all history as our finest hour. We suffered incredible disasters. We sustained unparalleled betrayals. We ran stupendous risks. We took upon ourselves overwhelming burdens. We endured intolerable humiliations. We were flung into the very depths of grief.

But we carried on. Guided by the Hand of God and sustained by our own right arm, we came through the shadows of defeat into the sunlight of a nobler dawn.

The chapters of this book have been written week by week as the poignant drama of our finest year unfolded itself. They are not meant to be a narrative of events. They are an optimist's view of the war, and are gathered together as a record of the emotions stirring within us during these 366 historic days and nights.

the occasional buttered "hot cake" or jam pastie, but little did either the old man or the boy realise what long-term benefits their nightly rendezvous in the bakehouse were to reap. For even at such an early age Arthur acquired a keen interest in the Press in general and politics in particular. Adding this to the all-round love of the Bible which he learned at home and at Sunday School, the young lad achieved an intellectual and spiritual springboard which within little more than a decade were to catapult him to the top of Fleet Street and make him the foremost Christian journalist of the times.

Arthur was born on 21st July, 1875, at Stapleford, which lies some half-dozen miles south-west of Nottingham and almost on the Derbyshire border. His parents were staunch Nonconformists and leading members of the Baptist Church. The boy's father, an engineer in a local factory, was a deacon and carried out his duties "with unsmiling gravity and inflexibility of purpose". Such was his devotion to his church that Mr. Henry Mee wore parson's garb — broad-brimmed hat and long, black frock-coat — when travelling to or attending services, and he was flattered if folks mistook him for a minister of the church. Though considered something of an eccentric Henry Mee was a respected citizen and well known for his firm convictions and radical views.

As a boy Arthur attended the Stapleford Board School (later renamed in his honour). The young scholar was greatly influenced by the teachings of George Byford, the school's patriotic headmaster. It was Byford who instilled into him an undying love of England and the British Empire, with the result that Arthur Mee was to be a patriot all his life, a view reflected in much of his writing.

The engineer's son did not inherit any of his father's mechanical skills. As a schoolboy he loved reading and writing, but had little time for science and geometry. Neither did he care for sport or swimming, except in the company of his brothers and sisters. He much preferred the companionship of books.

In 1889 Henry Mee took his wife and ten children to live in Nottingham, six miles away, in pursuit of work. The same year saw 14-year-old Arthur take his first steps into journalism, as a copyholder with the *Nottingham Evening Post*. A copy holder was a boy who read aloud from the "copy" while the proof-reader checked each word for accuracy on the galley proof.

The Council House in the centre of Nottingham. When Arthur was 16 he began his career in journalism with the town's Express newspaper.

A few months later Arthur wrote his first news story. While attending a service at a local Baptist church he took out his pad and pencil and recorded the minister's sermon. After writing up his story he took it, not to his employers, but to the rival *Nottingham Daily Express*. He felt that the radical *Express* would be more in sympathy with the liberal preacher's views than the more conservative *Post*.

At 16, Arthur joined the *Express* to begin a four-year apprenticeship in journalism. The conditions of the apprenticeship demanded that he was "not to drink, gamble, waste his employers' time, or get married". With a weekly wage of 16 shillings none of these things was likely to happen! For this payment young journalists on the *Express* were expected to work a seven-day week reporting police courts, inquests, public meetings and concerts. So eager was Arthur to learn his craft that after only 18-months on the job there was no other reporter less than ten years his senior who could beat him at speed or accuracy with shorthand.

Arthur Mee earned a reputation in local newspaper circles with his reporting of Sir William Harcourt's visit to Derby in 1895. Harcourt was the Liberal leader in the House of Commons, and his speech was eagerly awaited by every radical in Nottingham. Though the town's leading

Everyone a millionaire

Perhaps you have never compared your wealth with Mr. Rockefeller's, but these millions of his that go rolling away, healing the sick, educating the ignorant, and making the world a happier place, are nothing compared with the wealth of those of us who read this.

Mr. Rockefeller's money is poor beside our wealth. He can count his sovereigns; his bankers can tell him any day how much he has to spend. But who can measure the wealth that Nature gives us all? If we measure our riches by counting up the hours and minutes Life gives us we find that we have something like half a million minutes in a year. True millionaires are we, and how are we spending our treasure?

What do you do with your millions of minutes, more precious than dollars and gold? The world has no esteem for a man who wastes a million pounds, but it is worse to waste a million minutes. Imagine the long, long roll of millionaires of time; every street and school and house and workshop has them, millionaires in these priceless minutes as they pass.

Think of a minute and all it may mean. You may make yourself immortal in it; you may give the world some great idea, invent some new thing, discover some great piece of knowledge, lift up some sad heart; or you may throw it away as if it were nothing. In some minute of inspiration the great leaders of nations have come to decisions that have changed the face of history.

So precious is this golden coin of Time, the fleeting minute, and we have millions of them; millions upon millions Time pays into our bank for us to use wisely and spend well. They bring us opportunity and power. Time ill-spent will make a rich man poor; minutes wisely used will bring a poor man treasure overflowing.

A.M.

Our men have not lived and fought and died for nothing. They have covered themselves in immortal glory; they have quickened in us that passion for our country that has long been all too silent. How can we remember them, how can we honour them, better than by living for the things they died for?

A.M. from *Wonderful Year*, 1943

We are born into our heritage; we came into our British freedom as we come into the sunshine, and we think it will always be there. So it shall be, but only because we fight for it — if not with guns, then with hands and hearts and brains. There is this difference between freedom and the sunshine — that the sun shines on us all by the will of God, but freedom grows where it is planted by the will of men.

A.M. from *Wonderful Year*, 1943

Liberal newspaper, the *Express* was notorious for penny-pinching when it came to paying expenses for out-of-town reporting, and as a rule local radicals were compelled to buy the Tory *Nottingham Guardian* to read reports of major speeches in other cities and towns.

True to form the *Express* sent only its young writer from Stapleford to cover this important event, while the *Guardian* despatched several experienced newsmen. Single-handed, Arthur Mee copied down Sir William's speech word-for-word as he spoke. Then he dashed to Derby railway station and caught the first train back to his office sixteen miles away. While travelling he transcribed most of the speech, then dictated the rest to a colleague once he reached Nottingham. The complete speech appeared in the next morning's early editions . . . and thanks to Arthur Mee's initiative and determination the *Express* could, for once, look its rivals in the eye.

While still only 20 Arthur was appointed Editor of the *Nottingham Evening News*, the publisher's afternoon sister paper. The *Evening News* was a four-page sheet taking all the items that could stand a second printing from the morning paper. These were filled out by news agency reports and late news from staff writers and correspondents. Young Arthur's day started early in an office shared with *Express* editor, Sir John Hammerton. He remained there editing the *News* until the final edition reached the streets around five in the afternoon.

Up to this time the young editor's writing had been solely for the local press. At Hammerton's suggestion Arthur tried freelancing for national journals. His first attempt — an anti-smoking article — was published in the popular *Tit Bits* magazine in 1896. Other articles followed, and soon he was writing almost a complete story every day as well as editing the *Evening News*. He was receiving between £15 and £20 a week from magazine features while earning a mere £2 weekly from his employers!

Sir George Newnes, publisher of *Tit Bits*, was so impressed by this energetic Midlands writer that he invited Arthur to join his London staff. Not one to miss a golden opportunity, he accepted at once. Before leaving Nottingham for Fleet Street Arthur met a girl from Yorkshire named Amy Fratson while holidaying in Skegness. Within a few months of starting work for Newnes the couple were married, on 6th March, 1897, and made their first home in London's Tulse Hill district.

After a period with the Newnes group of journals Arthur moved over to the prestigious *St. James Gazette* as a columnist. As a freelance with this paper he was able to supplement his 7-guinea fee with other work. In 1901 he became editor of *Black and White*, a sixpenny weekly.

Five, sometimes six, days a week he was in Fleet Street editing the *Black and White*, for which he wrote the leading articles. At six in the evening he returned home to Tulse Hill and wrote his two columns for the *St. James Gazette*. These were typed between dinner and the midnight post, so as to reach the *Gazette* in time for the first edition. He never failed once, all his contributions going straight to the printers without need for correction by sub-editors.

Fellow journalists were astounded that the young man from Nottingham could seemingly write on any topic he chose with accuracy and authority. This was achieved through Arthur Mee's vast collection of newspaper cuttings which he kept in a specially-designed cabinet. Said he: "It is a cabinet of a quarter of a million articles, paragraphs, notes and references, taken from newspapers, magazines and books". The cabinet was insured for thousands of pounds.

Arthur's writing was not confined to journalism alone. During his editorship of *Black and White* (1901-1903) he published four books — biographies on Joseph Chamberlain, Lord Salisbury, Edward VII and the political commentary, *"England's Mission by England's Statesmen"*.

In 1903 he joined Sir Alfred Harmsworth's publishing empire as features editor on the *Daily Mail*. This gave the ambitious and prolific writer ceaseless opportunities for creative feature writing and contact with leading authors of the day.

No doubt Arthur Mee could have gone on to edit one of the country's great national newspapers, such was his talent and capacity for hard work. Instead, he was to forsake adult journalism to become a children's writer, the like of which the world had never known.

Besides his newspaper empire Harmsworth was gaining a reputation as a publisher of first-class children's books. His success with the *Harmsworth Encyclopaedia* in 1905 encouraged him to print an entirely new work called the *Harmsworth Self-Educator*. He chose Arthur Mee to become its editor — a step that was to make the Nottingham newspaperman world famous.

Optimists Still

We found an old friend the other day nipping across the street to catch his train. He is 88, and he said, "I think you are not such an optimist as you were." It sets us thinking. Are we? Let us see why we always have been optimists.

The useless things of today are the blessings of tomorrow and no man can say what will happen; but always Life has gone forward to something better.

The reptile which was once the King of Earth would have seemed a useless and horrible thing then, but the reptile kept rivers sweet before man came with his laws of health and his sanitary systems. For millions of years light and warmth were pouring down on the earth, and men would have thought it wasted, but Nature, which knew that man was coming, saved it up for him as coal.

All through these years God was preparing for mankind, and the power that made the earth for man has not deserted him from then till now.

Think of the microbes; they could have made the earth unfit for man if they had not been checked. Who held this power in leash through all the ages? Think of the electricity with which the earth is highly charged. Who restrains and controls this appalling force?

It is the working in human life of powers outside the human race. God will not fling His thunderbolts about, or let loose His floods upon the earth, or send His storms and lightnings with messages to man; but He will use the weapons He has made to suit His purposes. He has given us the power to save the world, and as His partners we shall save it.

And so, young friend of 88, we are optimists still.

A.M.

Surprises for the Traveller in England

(compiled by Arthur Mee in 1939)

The timbers of the Mayflower are in a barn in a country lane at Jordans, Buckinghamshire, with William Penn sleeping at the bottom of the lane.

Two masts of the Mayflower are in a schoolroom in Abingdon.

Two crosses over 1,000 years old are in the cobbled market-place of Sandbach in Cheshire.

The oldest picture of St. George is on the walls of Hardham church in Sussex, painted by a Norman artist.

A yew tree at Darley Dale in Derbyshire was growing when the Normans built the church there.

Hot water is still coming from springs at Bath as it has come for thousands of years.

A Norman painting of Judgment Day is still on the walls of Chaldon church in Surrey.

(continued opposite)

The Roman Baths at Bath.

It was at this time that the Mee family moved from London to Kent. Since the birth of his daughter Marjorie, in 1901, Arthur Mee had been searching for a house in the country, for he felt that a child should grow up knowing the beauty of Nature. He found what he was looking for at Hextable . . . a large house with five acres of gardens and a tennis lawn. It also had a much-needed library for Arthur's growing collection of books.

It was here that the successful journalist's religious upbringing came into conflict with a section of the local community. He frequently visited the village post office to send articles and letters to London. He was dismayed to find that the post office doubled as an off-licence with beer and spirits being sold over the counter. The teetotal Arthur Mee objected strongly to this state of affairs.

He bought land nearby and built a new post office, with a library and tea-room attached. He then had the postal business transferred, and persuaded his old friend and schoolmaster, George Byford, to become the postmaster.

Arthur's former boss on the *Nottingham Daily Express*, Sir John Hammerton, had by now joined Harmsworth, and was put into harness with Arthur on the editorial staff of the *Self-Educator*. This tremendous publication was circulated fortnightly, each issue containing 136 pages of knowledge in words and pictures. It was a sell-out from its first edition in 1906. This was followed by the equally successful *Harmsworth History of the World* — "Ten thousand pictures of ten thousand years", was Arthur's proud boast.

Sitting at home one day writing at his desk Arthur was amused to hear Marjorie, then aged seven, pestering her mother with relentless questions. "Why is this? . . . What is that for?" asked the little girl. An exasperated Amy Mee exclaimed to her husband — "Oh for a book that answered all these questions!" This tired statement fired the educationist's imagination. A book of answers! Yes, why not? A *children's* encyclopaedia!

The first two-weekly edition of *The Children's Encyclopaedia* was launched on 17th March, 1908: another 51 issues were to follow to make the complete set. Between 1910 and 1946 the hardback volume version sold well over five million copies throughout the world!

A year before the outbreak of the Great War (1914–1918) Arthur and his family left Hextable for a brand-new home on a hilltop above the lovely village of Eynsford, near

Arthur Mee with his seven-year-old daughter Marjorie. She it was who gave him the idea for the Children's Encyclopaedia.

(continued from opposite page)

Anne Hathaway's cottage, Stratford-on-Avon.

Two bells old enough to have rung in Magna Carta still ring at Chilworth near Southampton.

In the doorstep of the church at Munslow in Shropshire is a brick from the Great Wall of China.

The oldest window in England, a Norman window with Norman glass, is at Brabourne in Kent.

In Winchester Cathedral is a bench on which Norman monks used to sit.

We have 20 Saxon churches older than Alfred.

The east window of Gloucester Cathedral is as big as a tennis court.

The little church at Corbridge, not far from the Roman Wall, has an arch built by the Romans and carried across the fields by the Saxons.

Anne Hathaway's cottage has an old bed that has never been out of its room for 400 years.

In the Toc H church of All Hallows-by-the-Tower we may see the walls blackened by the fires of Boadicea.

Four lamps in Trafalgar Square were on the Victory when Nelson died.

Sevenoaks in Kent. This house was lavish, with beautiful gardens that Arthur and Amy sometimes opened to the public. A summer house, set in the woods behind the house, was the tranquil corner in which he did much of his writing. Not that he needed quiet to continue his work. His daughter, Marjorie, said of her father: "He could write in a room full of people, all talking, and then turn and join in as though he had been listening to every word. Even on journeys, he would correct proofs. He never really stopped working."

During the war years Arthur was kept busy editing the children's magazine, *My Weekly*, and writing features for

CHILDREN'S NEWSPAPER

OVER 2,000 ISSUES

The last edition of the Children's Newspaper dated 1st May, 1965. Arthur Mee launched this publishing legend in March, 1919, and it continued for over 2,000 issues until long after his death in 1943.

A front page of the Children's Encyclopaedia with Marjorie Mee, the editor's only child, on the cover.

Always a true patriot, throughout the First World War Arthur Mee kept the Union Jack flying from his house at Eynsford.

Lloyd's Newspaper. Though not a war reporter he did visit the British front line at Ypres — and had a narrow escape when a German shell blew the town's historic Cloth Hall to pieces behind him.

With the war's end he set about creating the most exciting journalistic innovation of its day: *The Children's Newspaper*. His brainchild first appeared on the streets in March, 1919, and sold for three-halfpence. The policy of *The Children's Newspaper* was simple: it made Goodness "news" by choosing its items from the world's press, rewriting, and presenting them in a style designed to appeal to young readers. At its peak the paper reached a circulation of half a million.

When Arthur Mee celebrated his golden jubilee of 50 years in journalism in 1941 he told his young readers in the 11th October issue of *The Children's Newspaper*: "There is no life in the world that can compare with the writing man's if he believes in God and man, and loves his work".

Though engaged in the hectic publication of newspapers and magazines Arthur still managed to find time to write books. Between 1917 and his death in 1943 he wrote around forty children's books, and an equal number aimed at adult readership. His greatest literary achievement was his *King's England* series of travelogues. County by county it describes 10,000 towns and villages in forty volumes, many of which are still to be found on library shelves

In the summer of 1931 the West Kent Electricity Company sought permission to run a cable underneath the drive of Arthur Mee's house at Eynsford, and offered him a "wayleave" payment. Arthur refused, but said he would accept instead a single red rose. And so, every June until his death in 1943, he received a rose from the electricity company . . . here being seen presented by the WKE manager's daughter, Margaret Allbright.

today, and is regarded as a modern "Domesday Book".

By nature a quiet and shy person, Arthur Mee was fully aware that his instrument was the "pen and not the tongue". Though a splendid wordsmith on the printed page, he was no public speaker and once admitted being terrified of standing up before an audience.

In his fine biography fellow-editor Sir John Hammerton, who worked closely with Arthur through many years of journalism, wrote: "He exhaled the joy of life. His cheerfulness was infectious. Nobody could well stay gloomy in his company".

Arthur Mee died in May 1943 following an operation at King's College Hospital, London. He was only 67 and had been talking confidently to friends of new books he planned to write in the many years he envisaged that lay ahead of him. Such was his enduring youth and lively spirit that he never lost his sense of wonder at the world about him. He was a tireless crusader for the Christian way of life. But most of all he was an Englishman, and he fought the good fight to his last breath.

The Main Works of Arthur Mee

Joseph Chamberlain: A Romance of Modern Politics (1900); Lord Salisbury: The Record Premiership of Modern Times; King and Emperor: The Life-History of Edward VII (1901); England's Mission by England's Statesmen (1903); Arthur Mee's Gift Book; The Fiddlers; The Parasite; S.O.S. (1917); Defeat or Victory?; Who Giveth Us the Victory? (1918); Little Treasure Island (1920); Every Child's Creed; Arthur Mee's Hero Book (1921); Arthur Mee's Golden Year (1922); Arthur Mee's Wonderful Day (1923); The Children's Bible (1924); One Thousand Beautiful Things; Arthur Mee's Talks to Boys; Arthur Mee's Talks to Girls (1925); The Children's Life of Jesus; The Pocket Bible; The Children's Shakespeare (1926); The Book of Everlasting Things (1927); The Children's Hour (1928); The Loveliest Stories in the World; The Children's Bunyan (1929); Arthur Mee's Story Book (1930); Jesus Said (1931); God Knows (1935); They Never Came Back; Dreams Come True; Heroes of the Bible; Heroes of Freedom (1936); Salute the King; One Thousand Famous Things (1937) The Rainbow Books: Shall We Live Again?; Life Calls to Youth; Good Morning Young England; One Hundred Lovely Things; Our Life's Star; Little Brother Ishi; The Broken Dream of Wilbur Wright; Christ Passing By (1938); Why we Had to Go to War; Arthur Mee's Blackout Book (1939); Arthur Mee's Book of the Flag; Call the Witnesses; Nineteen-Forty (Our Finest Hour) (1941); Immortal Dawn (1942); Wonderful Year (1943);

In additon to the above, his edited works included the Harmsworth Self-Educator (1905-7), History of the World (1907-9), The Children's Encyclopaedia (1908-10), The World's Great Books (1909-10), The Children's Treasure House (1926-28) and, of course, The King's England series (1936-45).

This England

This England is a quarterly magazine for all those who
love our green and pleasant land.

ACKNOWLEDGEMENTS

PHOTOGRAPHS

J. Allan Cash page 108; Keith Ellis page 125; Iris Hardwick page 120; E. Emrys Jones pages 33, 41, 86; Molly Jones page 107; Dennis Mansell page 75; Hugh Martineau page 114; Bill Meadows pages 35, 36, 91, 143; Jane Miller pages 74, 88; Tom Parker page 61; Cleland Rimmer page 12; Clifford Robinson page 31; John Tarlton pages 89, 111; M. & M. Teal pages 32, 37; Welsh Tourist Board page 138; M. Wright page 83.

We are grateful to the following people for their assistance in the preparation of this book: David Lazell for the chapters on Romany and Flora Klickmann; Betty Walthew (Sheila Kaye-Smith); Desmond Dunkerley (John Oxenham); Malcolm Griffin (Arthur Mee); James M. Charlton (Francis Brett Young); and the Reverend Brian Kingslake, nephew of Flora Klickmann, for kindly providing us with information and photographs.